The Dietitian Revolution

From Pink Collar to Power Players — A Call for Dietitians to Lead the Way in Preventive Medicine

WENDY LEONARD, MS, RDN, LDN

ISBN: 979-8-9997481-2-6

DEDICATION

To my fellow dietitians —

You chose this path because you believe in the power of food, the science of prevention, and the potential of lifestyle medicine to transform lives. You recognized the importance of this work before the world fully did — and you stepped forward anyway.

You've devoted years to making a difference, even on days you questioned your impact. Remember: you *are* making a difference. Stay the course and keep your spirit alive, because our field is one of the greatest in healthcare.

You are innovators, educators, and leaders. You translate science into hope, guide patients through transformation, and help them see what's possible — in their lives, their families, and their futures.

You are the change-makers our healthcare system needs. Every day, you prove that food is medicine, prevention is powerful, and evidence-based care transforms lives.

You are not optional. You are essential — the future of healthcare.

This book is for you: for the long nights, the creativity, and the quiet moments of doubt met with courage. It's for the revolution we're building together.

Because we're not here to follow.
We're here to lead. Let's go.

CONTENTS

INTRODUCTION

This book is about how we, as dietitians, can lead the future of preventive medicine — instead of watching it unfold without us.

No one understands the human side of healthcare the way we do. We've sat across from patients, offered them safety and compassion, and walked beside them through change. We've seen firsthand that when people receive personalized, evidence-based nutrition care, outcomes improve, costs decrease, and lives are transformed.

That's why I built my practice — and why I've worked to grow it into a thriving, collaborative model of care. Through hybrid one-on-one and group medical nutrition therapy programs, we've made care more accessible, engaging, and effective. Along the way, we've partnered with hospitals, physicians, corporations, and public health organizations — building a network grounded in one mission:
to unburden the physician, enrich the patient experience, improve outcomes, and reduce healthcare costs — through evidence-based nutrition led by registered dietitians.

But our vision must reach further. Dietitians are uniquely trained in nutrition and lifestyle medicine. We have the knowledge and compassion to help patients heal — and the power to transform healthcare itself. It's time for medical nutrition therapy to become a cornerstone of care, not an afterthought.

We must claim our seat at the table — as innovators, collaborators, and advocates. We must design care models that are high-touch, deeply personal, and proven to drive better outcomes. And we must ensure dietitians are valued and compensated for the impact we create.

At the heart of it all is legacy. The work we do today will define a future where patients thrive, healthcare is stronger, and our profession stands in its rightful place — recognized as essential.

This book is both a roadmap and an invitation. Together, we can redefine preventive medicine and transform the future of dietetics.

1 FINDING MY FUEL

I didn't become a dietitian to run a business. In fact, that was the farthest thing from my mind.

I became a dietitian because I experienced, firsthand, the power of food.

Back in high school, I was a runner — but not by choice. I had tried out for the soccer team my freshman year and got cut in the final round. I had no "Plan B." Running seemed like something anyone could do, so I joined the cross-country team with a few of my friends.

I kicked off the season with my first 5K race. I hadn't trained at all, aside from a few short sprints during soccer tryouts. But I had an older brother. So, what I lacked in preparation — I made up for with grit.

The gun went off, and I shot straight to the front of the pack. At the half-mile mark, I was a solid 100 yards ahead of the girl in second place.

My dad was at that race with his camcorder: a bulky 1980s video recorder that was about the size of a toaster. You can see my big smile and confident side glance as I run past my dad in that first stretch. From behind the camera, you can hear him cheering, his voice full of pride and excitement.

The camera follows me around the course, zooming in as I lead the race. My dad keeps cheering. Though, at this point, I'm too far in the distance to hear him. Then the video suddenly goes blurry — you can tell he's trying to refocus the lens. When the picture refocuses, everything has changed.

I'm going slower. *Much* slower.

It's honestly cringeworthy thinking about this now, even though it has been so many years ago.

I was just past the first half-mile mark into the 3.2-mile race when I hit the wall. My lungs began to burn, my stomach cramped up, and my legs turned to lead.

I slowed to a trot, barely faster than a walk. It was only seconds before the rest of the pack was on my heels.

Then, they were flying past me on both sides. Like a macrophage taking over a virus, they were surrounding me on both sides, enveloping me before their pack swooped past me. I felt the breeze created by the united front of their bodies. I vividly remember how I felt like I was in slow motion as I watched them pass, their strides smooth and effortless.

My dad's camcorder captures it all. In the video, a few moments after my dad refocuses on his daughter in that moment, you can barely hear my dad softly say, "Oh."

It's almost like his brain is catching up with what his eyes are seeing. His daughter, who had been leading the race, now looks like she's in pain and on the verge of falling. And then — the video stops.

I'm pretty sure he stopped recording out of kindness, sparing me the humiliation of having my entire implosion saved for eternity. Or maybe he was worried and went to check on me.

But the next clip starts after I've crossed the finish line. A group of red-cheeked girls — my teammates — are laughing, gulping water from plastic cups, and replaying the race amongst each other. My dad zooms in on me.

I'm not laughing. I'm bent over, hands on my thighs, ponytail flipped forward, staring at the grass. And then I hear him call out:

"Hi, honey."

I look up, exhausted and depleted, but somehow manage to roll my eyes. Not at him, but at myself.

"I know, Dad," I wanted to say without saying it.

Then you see his hand come into the frame, patting my back awkwardly as I'm still bent over.

"Good try, honey," he says, his voice carrying that mix of pep and pain only a parent can muster — the pep to lift me up and the pain of seeing me hurting, physically and emotionally.

And it was painful. Not just physically — though my stomach churned for a good ten minutes after the race — but emotionally, too. I was embarrassed by my overconfidence. I felt like I had let down my coach, my teammates, my dad, and myself.

But here's the thing: that race taught me something at thirteen years old.

I was never going to let that happen again.

I was going to figure out how to get to the front of the pack — and stay there.

And I did.

It didn't happen overnight, but week by week, I made changes. My dad had always been into health and had even taken a nutrition course in college. We grew up in a house without junk food, soda, candy, or even white bread. I remember going to my friends' houses and thinking I had landed in heaven when they had Lucky Charms or Kool-Aid.

But after that race, everything shifted. I started listening to my dad's nutrition lectures instead of rolling my eyes. I began cooking, experimenting, and reading books about nutrition for athletes — especially runners. I loved what I was learning, and even better, I started putting it into practice.

And things began to change.

Running started to feel good. My lungs didn't burn. My legs felt strong. I could run six miles while laughing and talking with friends. My anxiety started to ease. I became more focused in school. My grades improved. I was happier. And I was finally running with the best girls on the team.

By the end of the season, I was in the top five on my team. My coach was proud of me. My dad was proud of me. And for the first time maybe ever, I was proud of myself.

Other than one injury my junior year, I ran every season of cross country and track in high school — all three seasons, year after year. I maintained my healthy habits, pushed myself, and ended my senior year running my personal bests.

And somewhere along the way, I decided I wanted to study nutrition in college. I didn't know exactly what I'd do with the degree, but I knew one thing for sure: I was passionate about the way food had transformed my performance, my mental health, and my life.

My parents were supportive, and before I knew it, I was off to college, ready to learn everything I could about nutrition — and to figure out what kind of future I could create with it.

I couldn't wait.

Looking back now, I see that race as more than just a childhood memory. It planted the seed for everything that came next — my curiosity, my drive, and my belief that what we eat has the power to change everything: our energy, our mood, our health, our lives.

I didn't know it then, but this experience would shape my calling. It led me to nutrition, to becoming a dietitian, and eventually to creating something bigger than myself — a practice, a vision, and a movement dedicated to proving what I learned that cross-country season.

When we fuel the body right, we change the trajectory of health.

That belief is at the heart of everything I've been building since then. And as you'll see in the coming chapters, it's also at the heart of where we — as dietitians — are headed next.

REFLECTION

Every dietitian has a story about how they got here — and, at some point, many of us question why we stay. Take a few quiet moments to think about your own path:

1. What first inspired you to become a dietitian?

2. How has your experience in the field so far matched — or fallen short of — the vision you once had?

3. Have there been moments when you've felt disconnected from your purpose, like you were just "checking boxes" instead of changing lives?

4. What patients, experiences, or turning points have reminded you why this work matters?

5. Looking ahead, what would it mean for you to build a career that truly aligns with your values and passion?

This is your opportunity to pause and reconnect with the deeper "why" behind your work — the reason you chose this path and the purpose that still drives you today.

2 REALITY CHECK

I love what I do.
I love being a dietitian.
I believe it's the best career in healthcare.

But I didn't always feel that way.

A few years into my career, I started going to therapy — not to work through childhood trauma, but because I was ready to change careers.

That's right. Three years in, I was already miserable.

The Basement Years

I started my career as an inpatient dietitian at a hospital, hopeful and optimistic. I was excited to finally use everything I'd learned, to make a difference, to help people heal.

But reality hit fast.

The "Nutrition Services" office was buried in the bowels of the hospital, deep underground with no windows. To get anywhere, we had to walk through a series of cold, dimly lit tunnels just to reach the elevators that took us up to the patient floors.

Each morning, after a few minutes of commiserating with a dozen other twenty-something dietitians, I'd print my list of patients and assign priority to each one. Protocol said I'd see the sickest first. On average, I was expected to see twenty-five patients a day.

I grabbed my patient list, gathered my reference notebooks, and hit the floors.

Dietary Days

"Excuse me," I said gently to the nurse, her elbow resting on the patient chart I had just spent the last ten minutes searching for. I pointed at her elbow. "Could I borrow that chart?"

She rolled her eyes at the nurse next to her and handed it to me without saying a word.

The other nurse looked at my badge. "Oh, you're from *dietary?*"

"Yes, I'm the *dietitian*," I replied, forcing a smile.

"Great. Can you talk to the patient in room 504? She's complaining about the food."

"Uh… sure," I said, as politely as I could.

Make that *twenty-six* patients.

Checking Boxes, Not Changing Lives

Next stop: the cardiac floor. I had a consult. The patient was about to be discharged, but first needed to "see the dietitian".

The box needed to be checked.

I walked into the room and saw a man in a hospital gown, sitting on the edge of the bed, hunched over, clutching a red, heart-shaped pillow. They gave those pillows to patients after open-heart surgery to brace their fragile chests for the coughs and sneezes. It did little to subdue the pain of what felt like their sternum might split open again.

He looked up at me, his face pale and drawn. He was exhausted.

"Hi, my name is Wendy," I said softly, stepping closer. "I'm a dietitian, and I'm here to talk to you about the heart healthy diet."

His shoulders sagged, and his face sank.

"I know you don't feel well," I said, handing him a brochure, "but we need to go over this before you leave."

I proceeded to cover the heart health diet: saturated versus unsaturated fats, the importance of fiber, healthier cooking methods, how to lower sodium, etc.

His eyes were closed and his head bobbed for most of it.

Check. Now he could go home.

Losing Myself

Day in and day out, it was the same.

I was supposed to feel fulfilled, but instead, it was mind-numbing. I couldn't take it anymore. This wasn't what I had signed up for.

I became a dietitian because I believed in food as medicine. I wanted to help people heal, to witness transformation, to see lives change. Instead, I was walking the quiet halls alongside death, apologizing for disturbing patients and nurses. Crossing patient names off my to-do list, but not feeling like I had done anything productive.

And somewhere along the way, I began to lose myself.

I was done.

A Different Kind of Shift

But, while I was going to therapy and exploring career options, something else was happening. Something bigger.

I was a newlywed, and I was expecting.

I was ecstatic. Becoming a mom was something I had always dreamed of.

I had wanted to be married and have babies more than anything in the world.

And just like that, my career change could wait.

REFLECTION

There are seasons in our careers when we lose ourselves — when the work feels like box-checking instead of life-changing. When the passion that once fueled us starts to fade beneath the weight of protocols, quotas, and expectations.

Take a few moments to reflect on your own path:

1. Has there been a time when you felt disconnected from your purpose — like the work didn't match the vision you once had?

2. What moments, patients, or experiences have reminded you why you started in the first place?

3. If you could redesign your career around your deepest values, what would it look like?

4. How can you reconnect today — even in small ways — with the passion that first brought you here?

Sometimes, losing ourselves is part of the journey. But rediscovering our "why" is what allows us to create work — and lives — that truly align with who we are.

3 BREAKING POINT

Fast forward eight years.

We had just moved across the country — from Colorado to Rhode Island. I was excited to live near the ocean again. My oldest son, Jack, was eight. My youngest, Max, was three.

I had spent the previous eight years working part-time, keeping one foot in the door with my career while my main focus was on keeping my children alive — quite literally, at times. I had four kids in five and a half years. Chaos doesn't even begin to describe it.

My husband was traveling more than two hundred nights a year, and I was in charge of everything — the schedules, the schools, the meals, the meltdowns — everything, except supporting the family financially. That was all him. I was bringing in about four hundred dollars a week before taxes. Working gave me a break from the endless demands of motherhood, but my career aspirations were still on hold.

A New Beginning — Or So I Thought

Once the kids were settled into their new schools and activities in Rhode Island, I found a job at a private practice in Providence. And I loved it.

I was energized by the patients who came in looking for guidance with their health. I was using one of my greatest strengths — listening. I loved hearing their stories, giving them a safe space to share and heal. I loved asking questions, gathering all the pieces, and shaping them into thoughtful, individualized nutrition and lifestyle plans.

My patients inspired me. Many came back thrilled to share what they had accomplished since our last session. Others were frustrated, stuck, struggling to change. And I did everything I could to help them figure out why. Most of the time, it wasn't the meal plan, the strategy, or the science holding them back.

It was the person staring back at them in the mirror.

I had been working part-time at the practice for almost two years when my world started to fall apart.

At first, it wasn't my world — it was my marriage. But, truthfully, it had been unraveling for years. We had been in couples counseling for most of our marriage. That's never a good sign. But with four little kids and a husband who traveled more than half the year, I kept forging ahead.

When Everything Crumbled

As time went on, the relationship became more painful, and it became clear I needed to think about what was best for my children. It wasn't just about me anymore.

I had no idea how I was going to make it as a single mom of four. I was working two days a week, making thirty dollars an hour — ten years into my career and with a master's degree. I started looking at full-time hospital jobs as a clinical dietitian, but with four kids in four different schools — two of them in half-day programs — I couldn't figure out how to make it work.

I had no family nearby to lean on. I was paying my babysitter twenty-five dollars an hour. Anyone can do that math. It wasn't pretty.

And so, the thought crept in:
Maybe I should have just stayed.

That sentence haunted me more times than I'd like to admit.

It sounds counterintuitive, but at times I convinced myself that staying — keeping my head down, keeping the peace, compartmentalizing — might have been easier than the hell I was going through.

Because leaving meant walking straight into a tsunami: the brutal chaos of family court, the legal custody battle, and the constant confrontation with a man whose anger and volatility only intensified once I decided to leave.

But on the days when my head was clear, I knew I had made the right decision.

The Breaking

I didn't know how I was going to make it. But I knew I would.

That season of my life was full of stories I may share someday in another book. This isn't that book. But I will tell you this: as horrific as that time was, I experienced moments of peace and clarity in the midst of the worst time in my life.

I began having glimpses — memories, visions, and moments I couldn't explain. A memory of my mom as a child. A sense that my maternal grandmother, who had passed away years earlier, was with me — giving me signs that I was on the right path. I even knew, without doubt, that my children had a guardian angel — my friend's seventeen-year-old son, who had passed away just a few years earlier from an accidental overdose, just a stone's throw from our house.

Those glimpses came almost daily. They helped me understand why I was going through this — that the past and the future of my family were divinely connected, and that I was not alone in breaking the generational cycle of abuse and trauma.

When you hit the lowest point of your life, there's nowhere else to look but up.

I was broken. In those moments of total hopelessness, I cried out — not just for myself, but for my children. I pleaded for their lives. I pleaded for my own.

There were days I couldn't even form the words to ask for help. All I could do was cry. What I experienced then helped me to understand that crying, in itself, was a prayer — the soul asking for help in its rawest, most honest way.

I wept — for myself, for my kids, and for strangers I saw in the courthouse every week, carrying heartbreak for themselves and their children just like mine.

I yelled at my ancestors — not the ones still living, but the ones long gone. I was furious at them. Furious that they had failed to stop the cycles of trauma and abuse, but had perpetuated it instead. I hated that they went to their graves without fighting for themselves or their children and grandchildren, leaving the next generations to carry the weight of their wounds.

I asked God:
Why me?

I had always worked hard on myself. I had tried to do better, to protect my children from what we had experienced, to stop the generational trauma from creeping into their lives.

But it had. Now they had been exposed to it, too. I had failed to protect my children. *I had failed as a mother.*

And it only made the exposure worse when I did the one thing I thought would save them.
When I left.

I even yelled at God:
Why didn't You help me protect my children from this?
I can handle it, but why them? They are so little. So innocent.

The Soul Cracks Open

And then something happened.

When you reach the point where you cry out from your soul — not from physical pain, but from spiritual pain — something inside you breaks.

And if you allow it to fully break — to crack wide open — everything you thought you knew about your life, about the people in it, and even about yourself spills out and shatters around you. And in that moment, you are not, and you never will be, the same person you were before.

At least, that's how it was for me.

I began to realize that I was walking through hell on earth. Yet I felt more connected to God and heaven than ever before. I experienced unexplainable peace — even joy at times — as I confronted the darkness. I surrendered everything I knew and loved on this earth. I pleaded for God to intervene — to save us.

In the rawest and most desperate of moments, as I cried out for help, I experienced something I will never forget. I saw, in some way, my prayers breaking through the invisible barrier between heaven and earth. There, on the other side, were angels receiving my prayers.

In that moment, I knew that even though I couldn't protect my children on earth the way I wanted to, they were protected. And the protection and love surrounding them were greater than anything I was capable of — greater than anything I could ever comprehend.

Even now, at the end of my most desperate prayers, I still say, "Boom!" Then I lift my arms, look up, and declare, "It is done!" — and in that moment, I know it truly is.

(Admittedly, it might look a little crazy to anyone watching. But that's the thing about faith — most of its greatest acts do look a little wild from the outside.)

A Door Opens

Two months later, I still had no plan for income. I had even accepted the possibility that I might lose everything — even my home. And strangely, I was at peace with it.

One afternoon, a friend asked me to tag along while she toured an office space in a professional building near my house. I went with her, just to help her decide.

While we were there, the woman showing us the space asked about my work. I shared a little about my situation. She was around my mom's age — warm, kind, and attentive. She listened closely.

Then she shared her own story. Her husband had been killed in an accident when she was pregnant with their fourth child. She told me how hard it had been; but also how, in time, everything worked out. Her words comforted me in a way I didn't know I needed.

And then she asked:
"Are you interested in an office space?"

Around the corner was a small, empty office.

I went to see it.

This is what happens when something inside you has already broken —
when you've completely surrendered.

You stop fearing failure.

Because when you've already lost the one thing you wanted most in life,
failing at anything else doesn't matter as much anymore.

But here's the thing: failure still wasn't an option for me.

I had four little people depending on me. They were watching me.
Listening. They had overheard the threats — the warnings that if I left,
we'd be homeless and without a penny.

They were counting on me.

And that was all it took for me to decide: I would not fail.

I didn't know how I was going to do it, but I knew I would figure out a
way to provide for them — even on a dietitian's salary. It meant
thinking differently, working creatively, and taking risks I never thought
I'd take. There was a fire inside me now — one I had never felt before.
I had a purpose to fulfill, and it was bigger than me.

Even though I didn't have all the answers, I had something else: faith.

I couldn't see the whole path ahead, but I believed I was being guided
by something greater than myself. It felt as though a light appeared just
bright enough to show me the next step. And when I took that step,
another appeared… and then another.

I couldn't see ten steps ahead. I couldn't even see two. But each time I
moved forward, I trusted the light to guide me. I had never lived in
faith like this before. To this day, I still call them my "faith steps".

There's something incredible about living this way — knowing, deep in your soul, that there is more than what we can see here on earth. That there is something greater we can lean on, trust, and surrender to.

So, I signed the lease.

And that little office — with its blank walls and quiet stillness — became the first space where I could start to rebuild my life.

REFLECTION

Life has seasons that break us open, revealing parts of ourselves we didn't know existed. Sometimes, what feels like the end is really the beginning — but we rarely see it until we take the first step forward.

Take a moment to reflect on your own journey:

1. Think back to a time when life felt like it was falling apart. What were you being asked to surrender, and what strength did you discover in the process?

2. Have you ever experienced a moment when you took a leap without knowing how it would all work out? What guided you forward?

3. What role has faith — whether spiritual, personal, or intuitive — played in your biggest life transitions?

4. What "faith step" could you take today — a small, intentional action that brings you closer to the life or purpose you feel called to build?

Sometimes, the light only shows us one step at a time. But when we trust it — and take that next step — we are carefully guided to the place we were meant to be.

4 DAY ONE

I started small. Just me.

Sitting in my new office — a tiny, windowless room that somehow felt both full of possibility and completely terrifying. One of my friends had given me a prayer plant to celebrate this new chapter. It brightened the room, but I wasn't sure how it was going to survive without sunlight. Honestly, I wasn't sure how I was going to survive either.

I had a marketing plan — sort of. My "strategy" was to visit a few medical offices in the area and introduce myself. I didn't want to do it. There was a reason I hadn't chosen marketing as a major. But I had no choice.

My mom had been a business owner too. She was a physical therapist and opened her own practice when I was in high school. I remembered her telling me how she went to doctors' offices with prescription pads that had her name printed across the top. She wanted to make it easy for physicians to sign the slip and hand it directly to the patient. That's how she started growing her business.

I knew times had changed and this approach was a little outdated, but some of the doctors were older, and I figured they might appreciate the gesture — even if referrals were now being faxed from their offices.

So, I did what she did: I had my own prescription pads made.

My First Attempt at Marketing

I also wrote a letter to providers, letting them know I was starting my practice and that I wanted to help them, their patients, and even their staff. This became my golden ticket.

I brought folders stuffed with my marketing materials and, yes, I walked into these offices cold. No introductions, no invitations. I was basically soliciting.

But I didn't show up empty-handed.

I brought little party favor bags filled with Godiva dark chocolate and organic green tea. The ladies behind the front desks were curious immediately. And when I offered a free nutrition consultation for anyone on their staff, their faces lit up.

Suddenly, conversations started. At least one person in almost every office admitted they had been thinking about getting healthier and said she'd probably take me up on my offer. There was an energy in the room — a ripple of excitement I hadn't expected.

At one office in particular, we were laughing and chatting when one of the primary care physicians, Dr. K, walked in to see what all the commotion was about. The staff introduced us, and he immediately started asking me questions:

"What exactly does a dietitian *do*?"
"What would you work on with my patients if I referred them to you?"

As I explained my approach, I could see his wheels turning. He was interested in nutrition personally, but had never even considered referring his patients to a dietitian.

The Turning Point

The conversation wrapped up, and I walked out of the medical building relieved that my marketing for the day was done.

Less than an hour later, I had a notification that I had received a fax. I logged into Healthie, my electronic healthcare platform.

There it was: my first patient referral — from Dr. K.

And then another came in. And another. By the end of that afternoon and into the early evening, I had seven new patient referrals from one doctor.

And they didn't stop coming.

Dr. K started getting positive feedback from his patients — and the results were showing up in their labs, their weight, and their symptoms.

Soon, his partner began referring his patients to me, too.

With one morning of marketing and one primary care physician willing to take a chance on me, my business was growing.

Rooted and Growing

Weeks later, as I sat in my tiny office, my eyes landed on my prayer plant — perched on the small table next to the chair where my patients sat.

Sometimes, a leaf would suddenly pop up while a patient was talking, and we'd both laugh at the timing. But one day, something happened that I'll never forget.

A patient was sharing an emotional story when one of the largest leaves slowly bent downward, right where the stem meets the leaf, until the tip rested gently on her shoulder. She stopped mid-sentence, startled, and looked at the plant, then back at me.

For a moment, neither of us spoke. We just stared at each other with wide eyes, completely silent.

And then — almost as if we were looking into a mirror — we both broke into smiles. Seconds later, we were laughing. The kind of laugh that only happens when you witness something so unexpected and magical that you know, instantly, it's a once-in-a-lifetime moment. And that you've just shared it with someone who, from that day forward, could never be considered a stranger again.

Despite the lack of sunlight, my prayer plant was thriving. Every morning, I'd arrive to find new leaves and ones ready to unfold.

This day, I was noticing how its leaves stretched outward, reaching for something that I couldn't quite see.

Despite the lack of natural light in my office, it was growing stronger by the day.

And in that moment, I realized — so was I.

REFLECTION

Before moving on, pause and connect this chapter to your own journey. Starting something new is never easy — but those first steps often shape everything that follows.

1. When you first started your work as a dietitian, what emotions came up for you — fear, excitement, uncertainty, hope?

2. Who took a chance on you early in your career, and how did that shape your path?

3. Think of your own "prayer plant moments" — those unexpected signs, conversations, or connections that reminded you you were on the right path. What were they, and how did they make you feel?

Take some time to reflect on where your journey began and how far you've come. Write down your accomplishments, big and small. Take a moment to celebrate what you have accomplished. Sit with this list for a little while longer. You can be proud of yourself. Put this list somewhere you can see it daily, a powerful reminder that you are a change-maker.

5 ILLUSION OF CARE

She sat across from me — a 52-year-old woman named Leslie — tears rolling down her cheeks. Her primary care doctor had just put her on four new medications: two for high blood pressure, one for reflux, and one for high cholesterol.

When I asked her what her doctor had said about changing her diet or lifestyle, she shook her head.

"He just told me to stop eating carbs. Specifically, anything white. When his nurse came in, she joined the conversation and told me to read a book called *The Obesity Code*. She said she lost twenty pounds in two months by eating just one meal a day. I think she was waiting for me to congratulate her, but I couldn't even speak. I walked out of the office crying. It was awful."

Four prescriptions — and a whole lot of bad nutrition advice later — here she was, sitting in my office, searching for the truth.

A Broken System

The part that haunted me most was that Leslie wanted to change. She came to her first appointment desperate, frustrated, but ready to do the work. And yet, not one healthcare provider had given her the time, the tools, or even the option to improve her health through anything other than medication.

That was the moment I began to see the truth:
Our healthcare system isn't built on wellness — it's built on illness.
It thrives when we stay sick. Profit margins rise as we become even more sick.

What kind of healthcare system have we built, if it is only profitable when human health declines?

I don't blame the doctors. Most are doing the best they can. But the reality is this: most doctors don't have the time to truly listen, connect, and create personalized plans. Instead, they're left with a prescription pad and ten to fifteen minutes per patient.

The Illusion of Care

They're incentivized to show numbers improving — lower cholesterol, lower blood pressure, fewer symptoms. But no one talks about the bigger picture.

Cholesterol levels drop, yes — but few mention that our bodies need cholesterol to create the very hormones that protect our hearts and brains.

Reflux pain disappears with one pill — yet that same pill neutralizes the stomach acid our bodies need to digest food and protect us from harmful pathogens.

Blood pressure improves with one pill... then a second... then a third. The numbers look better on paper, but the side effects rarely make it into the conversation. Suddenly, a lingering cough demands daily over-the-counter meds, or a beta-blocker slows the heart so much that even a brisk walk feels like climbing a hill in wet cement. The legs grow heavy, the lungs protest, and the motivation that once came easily starts to fade.

The bandaids pile up, but the root cause is never addressed.

When You See It, You Can't Unsee It

Once you recognize the truth, you can't go back to unseeing it.

And if you're anything like me, something begins to stir — deep in your conscience, deep in your soul.

I did what I could.

I called referring doctors.
I asked for permission to bridge patients off reflux medications, using a combination of distilled aloe vera, digestive enzymes, and probiotics, while we worked on diet and lifestyle changes.

I asked physicians to order calcium score scans before starting patients on cholesterol meds — to confirm whether calcification was even present.

I had conversations with doctors about food, inflammation, and disease — and about how we could lighten their load with a single medical nutrition therapy referral.

I taught my patients, young and old, how to become their own health advocates.

They shouldn't have to — but if they don't, they risk their health… and their lives.

The Trap We're All In

In our healthcare system, we aren't preventing disease — at best, we're managing it.

A lab value creeps above "normal." A symptom lingers longer than a week. And before we know it, the flow of prescriptions begins.

But we don't feel better.
We aren't getting healthier.

Patients get trapped in a system designed to react, not restore.

And dietitians? We've been trapped, to. Relegated to the sidelines, undervalued and underutilized, even as the evidence for food-first care becomes undeniable.

REFLECTION

Leslie's story isn't rare. It represents thousands of patients caught in a system designed to manage disease rather than prevent it. As dietitians, we stand at a crossroads: we can either adapt to the way the system has always worked — or we can choose to disrupt it.

Take a moment to reflect on your role within this broken healthcare model:

1. Think about your "Leslie." Who is one patient whose story stays with you — the one that opened your eyes to how flawed the system really is?

2. When you hear patients talk about conflicting advice from doctors, apps, books, and friends, how do you approach rebuilding their trust in nutrition and in themselves?

3. In your current practice or role, are you operating reactively — following the system's rules — or proactively, creating your own path toward prevention and empowerment?

4. If you had complete freedom — no insurance restrictions, no productivity quotas, no systemic limitations — what would your ideal model of care look like?

When you begin to see the system for what it is, you also begin to see your power to change it. One patient. One practice. One step at a time.

6 GROWING PAINS

In the early days, I was simply focused on helping as many patients as I could. Then one of my dietetic interns asked, "Could I work for you?" I paused for a moment and said, "Okay, sure — we can figure this out." That one conversation marked a turning point. My business was no longer just me — it was becoming *we*.

I hired her once she became a dietitian. Soon after, I hired another dietitian. For the first time, the practice felt bigger than my individual caseload.

Pain — The Teacher

I was still seeing patients full-time, but now added onto that was training, mentoring, managing, creating policies and procedures, and learning on the go. I was balancing leadership and patient care while figuring out payroll, employer taxes, scheduling, office space and all of the other behind-the-scenes details of owning a business that no one teaches you in school.

But after the first full year, I ran the numbers.

Big lesson here — don't wait an entire year to run your numbers.

Despite all our effort and growth, the numbers didn't lie — we were *losing* money.

I remember sitting there, looking at the spreadsheets. I felt sick to my stomach as I realized something fundamental: hard work or growing a business doesn't always equate to more profits. In this case, it was the opposite.

The truth was, we were doing everything right from a care standpoint — but the system wasn't designed to reward that. Medical Nutrition Therapy only reimburses for face-to-face time. There's no reimbursement for charting, communicating with other healthcare providers, responding to patient messages, reviewing food logs, tracking progress, or entering outcomes data. All the invisible work that makes care effective — none of it is billable. When it was just me, it didn't matter. But now I was paying others for this time — and the numbers weren't adding up.

And then there were no-shows and late cancellations. Every missed appointment was a financial hit — not just for that hour I paid the dietitian — but for the time we could have filled with another patient.

Some weeks, it felt like we were spinning our wheels — fully booked on paper, but not meeting the numbers to sustain salaries, office rent, and operational expenses.

It was a wake-up call. The math simply didn't work. The traditional model wasn't built for dietitians to thrive. To make this work long-term, we needed a new approach — one that valued our time, protected our revenue, and rewarded efficiency without sacrificing care.

That realization changed everything. It forced me to stop thinking like a clinician trying to survive the system — and start thinking like a business owner ready to transform it.

The Fear Disguise

After that realization about reimbursement and revenue loss, I started to think differently. Around that same time, we hosted our first mini-retreats — Full-Filled. One of my favorite patients, Lori, attended.

During one of our group discussions, Lori shared that she was searching for purpose in her work. She was successful, earning a great salary at a corporate banking job, but she said something that struck me: "I'm not fulfilled." We talked about what it means to truly align your work with your values — how health, purpose, and joy are all interconnected.

Lori wasn't ready to make the leap yet, but that retreat planted a seed for good things to come.

Then, COVID hit. Everything came to a screeching halt. We had to shut down the office and cancel appointments. Patients were sick, and so were we. Telehealth had just been approved under the COVID emergency, but it was brand new territory. Patients weren't used to it — and truthfully, neither were we.

There were moments of real fear.

Am I going to have to let someone go?
Will I have to close the business?

But those thoughts didn't stay for long. I had already learned that when fear arrives — you have to face it, lift up it's ugly disguise, and look for the opportunity.

So, I made a conscious choice: *I accept the challenge.*

Still, I'd be lying if I said it was easy. Fear did creep in at times. Some nights, I stared at my bank account after payroll cleared and felt sick to my stomach. There wasn't always much left — and sometimes, nothing at all. The numbers didn't lie: I couldn't keep doing things the same way. Something had to change, or I was going to lose the business I had built from the ground up.

Plus, I still had four little people who were counting on me.

Shifting Directions

A few months after the shutdown, my phone rang — it was Lori. She had been let go from her corporate job because of COVID. Her voice was calm, but I could hear the uncertainty underneath.

"Wendy, I don't know what's next," she said. "Do you have any job opportunities?"

At that moment, I didn't. We were still finding our footing and rebuilding our business in a world that had turned upside down. Lori wasn't a dietitian, but she had a passion for wellness and was curious about becoming a health coach. I told her, "Let's figure this out. Maybe this is the start of something new."

I reached out to a few of my friends who were dietitians and health coaches to get advice on the best certification programs, and we landed on Wellcoaches. I suggested that Lori begin her certification while I tried to figure out what the next chapter could look like with her in it. I believed in Lori, her passion and her work ethic. I knew we would figure this out together.

At first, I had her help with patient communication between visits — checking in with encouragement, and accountability. But I quickly realized that without a sustainable financial model, this was another drain on our already thin margins. We needed to find a way for her role to generate revenue, not just add more costs.

So, we pivoted again. Lori and I started reaching out to corporations around Rhode Island to see if they were interested in employee wellness programs. A few were intrigued, but most already had contracts with large telehealth platforms like Virgin Pulse or Livongo. I began to see a pattern — the corporate wellness market was saturated. For now, at least, this door was closed.

I was doing research on the internet looking for ideas on how we could incorporate health coaching into our practice. That's when I stumbled upon something that changed everything: the CDC's Diabetes Prevention Program: *Prevent T2*. The Rhode Island Department of Health had received federal funding to expand this program for state residents. As a group dietetics practice, we were a perfect fit to deliver it.

I called Lori immediately: "This could be it!"

She began reaching out to the Department of Health, leaving messages and following up diligently — one message, then another, then another. For three months, we didn't hear a word. It was frustrating, but we didn't give up.

And then one day, the call came. They wanted to meet with us to discuss how we could begin offering the Prevent T2 program. That single conversation would open the door to an entirely new chapter in our business — one that aligned perfectly with our mission to help people live healthier, longer lives.

A New Path Forward

After that first meeting with the Rhode Island Department of Health, everything began to shift. We were officially invited to become part of a statewide network of providers delivering evidence-based diabetes prevention. The collaboration opened doors we hadn't even known existed — new referrals, new relationships, and new momentum. For the first time, it felt like we'd built a system that could truly work — one that let us do what we loved, reach more people, and operate with both purpose and stability.

Many of our patients had been asking for more structured group support, so Prevent T2 fit perfectly. It wasn't just another nutrition class — it was a lifestyle change program rooted in accountability, education, and connection.

We started seeing real momentum. The group setting allowed patients to learn from each other, celebrate wins, and feel less alone in their journey. For us as dietitians, it was energizing to deliver care in a way that was both impactful and scalable.

Everything is Negotiable

When we first joined the Prevent T2 program, our team was energized. The evidence was clear, the mission aligned, and we knew this work could change lives. What we didn't anticipate was how hard it would be to make it sustainable.

At first, we were reimbursed for our time, but not for billing — a well-intentioned structure that made the numbers look good on paper but didn't add up in practice. Within a few months, it became obvious that we were going to run out of money before the contract was up. Passion alone wasn't going to keep the business running.

So, we proposed a modification to our contract with the RI Department of Health: redirect the grant funds toward supports and incentives for participants and allow us to bill MNT directly through our own business. It was a risk — a departure from the original contract — but it made sense. When the Department of Health took it to the CDC, they loved it. The modification was approved, and with that single decision, everything shifted.

We now had a model that could grow.

Recognition and Resolve

In late 2024, our work began to catch the attention of people outside our usual circles. That November, we were honored with the *Grace Diaz Blue Light Award* from the Rhode Island House of Representatives — a recognition given to those advancing diabetes prevention and community health. It was an unexpected but deeply validating moment that proved that dietitians can take the lead — and the awards, when it comes to public health initiatives.

Around that same time, our persistence paid off in another way. After years of rigorous reporting, outcome tracking, and unwavering commitment to program integrity, Rhode Island Nutrition Therapy earned Full CDC Recognition for the Prevent T2 National Diabetes Prevention Program. It was the highest level of achievement possible— and one that few private practices ever reach.

That designation became a turning point. It validated our model as both clinically effective and financially sustainable, and it opened doors to national collaboration.

In October 2025, our team — along with our partners at Brown Health — was nominated for an innovation in healthcare award at the Diabetes State Specialist Summit in Atlanta, joining a community of innovators shaping the future of prevention.

Each milestone carried the same message: what we were building in Rhode Island was bigger than a single program. It was proof that dietitians could lead large-scale public health initiatives, redefine sustainability, and prove that compassionate, evidence-based care can thrive in the real world.

Those recognitions reminded us that credibility is earned not through titles or funding, but through outcomes, integrity, and the courage to keep building even when the path is unclear. They became our signal to refine what came next—to define our own standard of care.

Defining Our Standard of Care

What we learned through adding on our first Prevent T2 cohorts, was that these patients who were in our groups and seeing a dietitian for individual MNT were achieving the best outcomes. Not only that, they expressed how important the support in both the individual and group settings were to their success in making lifestyle changes.

That is when we committed to continuing to roll out the gold standard model — a hybrid standard of care that combines 1:1 Medical Nutrition Therapy (MNT) with group MNT programs to deliver high-touch, comprehensive support and the best outcomes.

In one-on-one sessions, patients work closely with their dietitian to create individualized nutrition and lifestyle plans. In group settings, they build skills, accountability, and community — learning from both their peers and our team of experts.

Our patients stay longer, connect more deeply, and achieve lasting results because they're supported through both individualized care and community connection. We're not reducing care to protocols; we're building relationships that last.

Creating a Financially Sustainable Model

As we refined this model, something else became clear — compassion alone doesn't sustain a business. To truly make an impact, our care model needed to be both clinically effective and financially resilient.

For years, dietitians have been caught in a system that rewards volume over value — reimbursed only for face-to-face time, while the real impact happens between visits. Our hybrid model changes that.

By blending 1:1 MNT with structured group programs, we maximize both outcomes and operational efficiency:

- 1:1 MNT sessions remain the cornerstone of personalized care, billed through insurance using CPT codes 97802 and 97803.

- Group programs — like *Prevent T2*, *Metabolic Weight Management*, *Total Lifestyle Change*, and *Nutrition Academy* — allow us to serve multiple patients while maintaining high-quality clinical care.

- Each group session is typically billable under group MNT code 97804 creating scalable, predictable revenue.

Financially, this means that instead of earning reimbursement for a single patient per hour, we can generate multiple units of value within that same time frame without compromising care, but enhancing it.

This model allows us to:

- Increase revenue per provider hour.

- Improve access to care by reducing per-visit costs.

- Strengthen outcomes through ongoing engagement which includes both provider and peer accountability, simultaneously.

- Reinvest profits into our team, technology, and community outreach.

- Support patients with MNT even if their insurance doesn't cover it. This is our definition of health equity (while continuing to advocate on the national and state level for health equity through legislation)

It's a model built to last — one that balances purpose with sustainability.

Our hybrid care model demonstrates that dietitians can lead healthcare transformation without burning out or sacrificing financial security. We've proven that it's possible to deliver compassionate, evidence-based care *and* operate as a thriving, forward-thinking business.

The best part? Our patients feel the difference — and so do our providers. Every decision, from program design to pricing, is built on the premise that we must continue to find the balance between financial sustainability and best outcomes. *The business cannot exist without both.*

REFLECTION

Before moving forward, take a moment to look back — not with judgment, but with curiosity. Growth often begins in the tension between what's working and what isn't. The moments of exhaustion, fear, or frustration in this chapter mirror the seasons every leader faces when stepping into something larger than themselves.

You may not have all the answers yet, but you're learning to ask better questions — and that's where transformation begins.

Use these questions to guide your reflection:

1. What "wake-up call" moments have you experienced in your own work or life? When did the numbers, the burnout, or the imbalance tell you that something had to change?

2. How do you typically respond when fear shows up disguised as logic or limitation? What might change if you started viewing fear as a signal for growth instead of a stop sign?

3. Think about a time when things fell apart — and something better emerged. What did that experience teach you about resilience or faith?

4. Who has believed in you during uncertain seasons? How can you honor or thank them — or pay that belief forward to someone else?

5. Where might you still be operating like a "clinician trying to survive" instead of a "leader ready to transform"? What small mindset shift could begin to change that?

6. What new approach or system could help you protect your energy, your time, and your mission more effectively?

Take a few quiet minutes to write down your answers. Let this reflection remind you that every struggle — every spreadsheet, every sleepless night, every uncertain phone call — was part of building something that matters. You're not just surviving the system; you're reshaping it.

7 A SHIFT IN PERSPECTIVE

Not long after we started our Prevent T2 groups and community outreach, Lori received a phone call that would change everything.

It was from Dr. D, a Doctor of Osteopathy who ran a private medical practice with her husband. Before COVID, she had a dietitian working in her office two days a week, but that dietitian had retired. She'd been trying to find a replacement ever since — someone who could help her patients make meaningful changes with food and lifestyle.

As Dr. D later told us, she had been searching through a file cabinet when something unexpected happened. A business card fell out and hit her right in the forehead. She picked it up — and it was Lori's.

Lori's months of outreach to physician offices had finally paid off.

After a funny conversation over the phone, Lori and I met with Dr. D the following week. Lori and I brought along flyers for our Prevent T2 and other group programs, ready to share what we were doing. But during that meeting, something even better happened.

Dr. D asked if we would be interested in renting office space in her practice. They would love to be able to have a dietitian "in-house" who could support their patients.

Dr. D explained that she was doing her best to help patients improve their eating habits, but it wasn't her area of expertise — and she didn't have the time to give it the attention it deserved. She wanted her patients to get professional nutrition care from dietitians, the experts in nutrition and lifestyle medicine.

That conversation marked the beginning of our first satellite office. And almost immediately, more referrals began flowing in. That first month, we had sixty-four patient referrals coming from Dr. D's practice.

Their patients loved it. They felt supported knowing that their doctor and their dietitian were part of the same care team — sharing information, speaking the same language, and working toward the same goals. It made them feel truly taken care of.

For us, it was another affirmation that collaboration — not competition — is the key to transforming healthcare. This wasn't just an office expansion; it was the start of a new way of practicing, one that wove dietitians directly into the heart of patient care.

Trust the Process

Around this same time, I made one of the most pivotal decisions of my professional life — I applied for and was accepted into the Goldman Sachs 10,000 Small Businesses program.

It was a 12-week intensive designed to help small business owners think strategically, build operational excellence, and create sustainable growth. The program was often described as an "MBA on steroids" for entrepreneurs — and it lived up to that reputation.

Every week, I attended classes one to two days per week, surrounded by other business owners from all industries — construction, retail, education, tech, and healthcare. We were all there for the same reason: to learn how to stop working *in* our business and start working *on* our business.

Each week focused on a new module, and together they formed a roadmap for transformation.

The 12 Modules that Transformed My Thinking

1. *You and Your Business*
    We started by looking inward — examining our leadership style, our purpose, and our "why." I realized that my business wasn't just a job; it was a mission-driven organization built to make an impact.

2. *Growth and Opportunities*
    This module pushed me to identify growth opportunities hiding in plain sight. I began to see how our programs and partnerships could scale beyond our current model.

3. *Money and Metrics*
   We dove into financial literacy — understanding the story behind the numbers. This was huge for me. I learned how to interpret financial statements beyond profit and loss, track cash flow, and project growth with data.

4. *Operations and Processes*
   We explored how to create systems that make a business run efficiently. I began building repeatable processes for scheduling, referrals, and patient communication that would later allow RINT to scale.

5. *Marketing and Customer Relationships*
   This was the turning point where I began to redefine who our *true* customer was. Up to that point, I believed our customer was the patient. But working through this module challenged that. When I reflected on our partnership with Dr. D, it hit me: our real customer was the physician.

6. *Understanding Your Market*
   I analyzed our competitive landscape and realized how underserved physicians were when it came to nutrition and lifestyle medicine support. Most dietitians were marketing to patients — few were positioning themselves as physician allies.

7. *Financing Growth*
   I learned how to strategically use funding, grants, and partnerships to fuel expansion rather than just cover expenses. This module inspired me to think bigger about future collaborations and diversified revenue streams.

8. *Being Bankable*
   This one was all about preparing your business to be seen as a credible, investable entity. I worked on formalizing contracts, creating clean financial reports, and tightening up our business plan.

9. *Leadership and Culture*
   I reflected on how to grow as a leader — how to mentor others, set expectations, and create a culture of accountability and purpose. It made me rethink how I was supporting my team.

10. *Growth Strategy and Action Plan*
    Each of us developed a written growth plan — a detailed roadmap to scale our business over the next 3–5 years. Mine centered on expanding physician partnerships and group programs that could reach more patients with fewer barriers.

11. *Performance and Implementation*
    We learned how to measure success — not just in revenue, but in outcomes, retention, and impact. I started tracking new metrics: patient progress, physician satisfaction, and long-term cost savings.

12. *Capstone and Pitch*
    The program ended with a formal presentation — our "Growth Opportunity Pitch." Standing there sharing my plan to build a physician-centered nutrition practice, I realized I was no longer just a clinician running a practice. I was an entrepreneur leading a movement.

By the time I graduated from the program, my mindset had completely shifted.

For years, I had viewed our patients as our primary customers. But through this experience — and through our partnership with Dr. D — I realized our true role was to serve the physician.

Doctors were our partners, not just referral sources. They needed us — to unburden them, to enhance the patient experience, and to improve outcomes in ways the healthcare system often failed to do.

That clarity changed everything.

Our mission at Rhode Island Nutrition Therapy evolved:

To serve physicians, enrich the patient experience, and improve health outcomes while reducing lifetime healthcare costs.

And who better to fill that role than dietitians? We are the experts in nutrition and lifestyle medicine. Physicians are overwhelmed and under-resourced — and we can help carry that weight.

The Goldman Sachs program didn't just help me refine my business. It redefined my purpose. It gave me the language, confidence, and structure to turn our practice into a scalable model for transforming healthcare — one partnership at a time.

There was a new vision at RINT, and now, it was time to put it into action.

From Vision to Action: The VIP Provider Program

Armed with my new perspective from the Goldman Sachs 10,000 Small Businesses program, I was ready to put our mission into motion. We had learned that our true customers were the physicians — and now it was time to build something that served them directly.

That's how the *VIP Provider Program* was born.
The concept was simple but revolutionary: make it *easy* for physicians to connect their patients with high-quality, evidence-based nutrition and lifestyle care — without adding to their already overwhelming workload.

We started by mapping what doctors told us they needed most: clear communication, trust, and follow-through. The *VIP Provider Program* would give them exactly that.

- Regular updates on shared patients — concise, relevant, and actionable.

- Simplified referral workflows that fit seamlessly into their routines.

- Group and one-on-one programs that extended their care plan between visits.

Our next partnership came through a group specializing in integrated medical weight loss. The timing couldn't have been better. The rise of GLP-1 medications — semaglutide, tirzepatide, and others — had changed the landscape of obesity treatment almost overnight.

Doctors everywhere were prescribing these new drugs, but many admitted they felt stuck when it came to nutrition guidance and long-term behavior change. Some were disregarding it altogether. Patients were losing weight quickly, but they still needed education on protein intake, muscle preservation, balanced meals, hydration, and mindset.

That's where we stepped in.

Through the *VIP Provider Program*, we partnered directly with an integrated medical practices to offer a coordinated approach — physicians managed the medical side, and we handled the nutrition and lifestyle piece. It became a true partnership.

We didn't just help patients optimize their results; we helped doctors feel supported, less burdened, and more confident knowing their patients were cared for comprehensively.

For RINT, this was the moment the vision became reality.
We were no longer just running a nutrition practice — we were helping reshape the way healthcare teams work together.

The *VIP Provider Program* became our bridge between medicine and lifestyle — and the blueprint for how dietitians could lead the future of preventive and integrative care.

REFLECTION

Before turning the page, take a few quiet moments to connect this chapter to your own journey.

Growth in leadership often begins with a shift in perspective—the moment we see our work through a new lens and recognize that true success comes from collaboration, not competition.

Let these questions help you explore your own turning points:

1. When was the last time you experienced a "business-card moment"? A coincidence, introduction, or open door that reminded you that timing and faith are often intertwined.

2. Who are your "Dr. Ds"? The partners, mentors, or allies who trust your expertise and invite you to grow alongside them. How can you nurture those relationships today?

3. What new clarity has emerged about who your *true* customer or audience really is? How has that realization changed the way you show up and serve?

4. Which area of your work still feels transactional instead of transformational? What small shift could you make to bring more purpose, partnership, or joy into that space?

5. How do you balance learning and leading? When was the last time you stepped into a program, course, or mentorship that challenged you to think bigger?

6. What does "collaboration over competition" look like in your world? How can you invite others to build with you rather than compete against you?

Take a few deep breaths and write down your answers.
You may find that the clarity you seek is already forming—just waiting for you to see it differently.

8 NEW CHALLENGES

There was another mindset that pushed me to the next level — one that came from an entirely different part of my life.

After going through my divorce, I saw firsthand the destruction that can happen in family court. Now, to be clear, there are many good and honorable lawyers who truly care about the how their job impacts the families, and the children, they represent — fortunately, my lawyer was one of those good men. But I also witnessed something darker: unnecessary trauma fueled by greed, power, and ego.

Because I had a good relationship with my lawyer, he shared with me about the "back-of-house" conversations that go on in the private suites at college basketball games and over glasses of expensive wine at the country club: "You take this one, I'll take the next". That refers to one spouse "winning" and the other one "losing".

I learned how they would fuel the fire between spouses when they knew there were more assets involved. That this would be the way to keep the money rolling in. A sustainable business at that. And the judges (former family lawyers) were in on it too. This made me sick to my stomach, because there are innocent children involved who are already suffering — and that makes them responsible for one of the saddest misuses of power imaginable.

What's even worse, is that this is one of the most dangerous times for children in terms of witnessing, or being a victim of violence. And they are increasing the risk during this critical time, for what has become just a game to them.

But for those going through a divorce, it can sometimes be a game of life and death. We've seen this before with one of our own. Several years ago, a dietitian in Rhode Island was the victim of a murder-suicide, while her three young children were home.

Mind Tricks

One day, as I sat there reflecting on it all, a thought struck me:

How much does a family lawyer make per hour?

I looked it up.
At the time, the average hourly rate was around $350 an hour.

And then came the next thought — the one that lit a fire in me:

As dietitians, look at all the good we are doing. We're helping people live longer, healthier, happier lives. We're bringing healing into the world — not harm. So why are we paid so much less than those creating so much destruction?

That question became my fuel.

I was determined to find a way for dietitians — the ones bringing good into the world — to earn what we're truly worth.

With Lori taking the lead, we began to add group MNT programs into the new standard of care at RINT. We were building a model that not only changed lives but was financially sustainable. Through the rollout of Prevent T2 and our Total Lifestyle Change (TLC) program, we were able to earn more than a divorce lawyer per hour — and we were doing it by *helping* people.

That realization was liberating. It wasn't about money for money's sake — it was about proving what's possible when purpose and profitability coexist.

We could do good, build abundance, and lift others along the way.

This mindset — believing that impact and income can grow together — became pivotal in how we continue to push the limits to new levels.

Realizing Our Value

For too long, dietitians have been conditioned to believe that our work is valuable but not *profitable*. That we should do it "for the love of helping people" — as if purpose and prosperity can't coexist. But I had seen the opposite. When we create real value, when we innovate, when we think like leaders — and when we understand the value we bring to the table — we can change lives *and* build a financially thriving businesses.

We don't have to work harder — we have to work *smarter*. We can leverage technology, collaboration, and innovation to build something bigger than ourselves.

It was never about leaving the heart of dietetics behind. It was about reclaiming it — about taking back the integrity, compassion, and science that our profession is built on and bringing it into a modern, financially viable structure.

Side note: I recently ran into my lawyer and when I told him about this chapter, he quickly informed me that the rate is now $500 an hour for family court lawyers.

No problem.

Scaling with Purpose

I realized that if Rhode Island Nutrition Therapy was going to continue growing, it couldn't depend on me — or on any one person. It had to be built on systems, not personalities. Structure, not chaos.

That's when the next phase began: scaling with purpose.

We started by bringing on more dietitians. The demand for our services — especially through our physician partnerships and group programs — was growing fast. It was both exciting and humbling to see our vision gaining traction. Each new dietitian brought fresh energy, new specialties, and a shared passion for lifestyle medicine.

But with growth came complexity. Managing schedules, compliance, payroll, and people was quickly becoming a full-time job on its own. That's when I decided to bring on Kristin, who stepped into the role of HR and Operations Manager.

Kristin brought the organization and efficiency we desperately needed. She helped develop internal systems, clarified job roles, implemented onboarding processes, and created accountability where things had once been informal. Having her on board was like finally being able to exhale — knowing that the details were being handled with precision and care.

Next, we expanded our Lifestyle Coaching Team. For a while, Lori had been running all of our group programs — from Prevent T2 to Total Lifestyle Change and Nutrition Academy — and it was simply too much for one person. By bringing in additional health and lifestyle coaches, we were able to reach more patients and expand our offerings while giving Lori the space to focus on leadership and program development.

With our programs running smoothly, the next big step was support at the front lines. We hired front office help — a small but mighty team to manage scheduling, calls, insurance verification, and patient communication. This was one of those behind-the-scenes changes that made a huge difference in our patient experience and overall efficiency.

Another shift came when we made the decision to bring billing in-house. Up until that point, we had relied on an external billing service. It worked — but it was disconnected. We wanted more visibility, more control, and a tighter workflow between the clinical and administrative sides of the business.

So we made the bold step: we brought billing inside RINT and integrated it directly through our EHR, Healthie.

It was a major investment in time, energy and resources. For several months, we were paying both our previous biller for services, as well as our in-house team, as we worked to ensure that everything was done properly. However, by owning our billing process, we improved accuracy, reduced lag time, and gained a deeper understanding of our financial health. Healthie became the central hub of our operations — linking patient care, documentation, billing, and data analytics all in one place.

For the first time, our operations felt aligned — like a living, breathing ecosystem where everything connected.

It wasn't easy. There were administrative bumps, tech glitches, and a learning curve that tested our patience. But we did it. And as we streamlined our operations, we built something even more important than systems — we built *stability*.

This was no longer a small nutrition practice. We were becoming a fully integrated healthcare organization — one that could scale, sustain, and lead.

Raising Up Leaders

As our team continued to grow and operations became more complex, I realized that my role needed to evolve again. I had spent years leading every part of Rhode Island Nutrition Therapy — from managing staff and mentoring interns to building programs and seeing patients myself.

But if the business was going to thrive long term, I couldn't be the one directing every decision. The systems were in place, the mission was clear — now it was time to develop new leaders who could carry that mission forward.

That's when I made the decision to promote Christina to Lead RD.

Christina had been with us long enough to understand our culture, our patients, and our vision for lifestyle medicine. She had consistently gone above and beyond — not just in her clinical work, but in her communication, initiative, and ability to support others on the team. She led by example — quietly, compassionately, and with unwavering professionalism.

I knew she was ready.

Promoting her wasn't about stepping away from leadership; it was about *sharing it*. I wanted to create a structure where leadership could be multiplied — where the next generation of dietitians could grow into roles that offered not only clinical fulfillment but also career advancement and ownership of their work.

Christina's new role allowed me to begin focusing more on the *vision* — exploring additional revenue streams, strengthening partnerships, and continuing to innovate — while she oversaw the day-to-day clinical flow and provided mentorship to newer RDs.

This shift was pivotal. It allowed me to step back from being the central hub of everything and start functioning as a true CEO — one who builds people, not just systems.

And it was deeply rewarding to watch Christina rise into her role with confidence, grace, and purpose. Seeing her lead reinforced everything I believed about the power of mentorship — that when you invest in people, they not only grow; they help the entire organization flourish.

At that point, Rhode Island Nutrition Therapy wasn't just *my* practice anymore. It was a living, evolving community led by a team of passionate professionals — all united by one mission: to transform health through food, lifestyle, and connection.

REFLECTION

This chapter marked a turning point — the moment purpose met power. It's where the realization took root that doing good and doing well are not opposites — they're allies. When dietitians recognize the true value of their impact, they stop asking for permission and start leading the way toward a new standard of care.

Take a moment to reflect on where you are in your own evolution: Have you ever felt undervalued in your profession — and what stories have you told yourself about what's "possible" for a dietitian to earn?

1. How do you define your worth — by the hours you work or by the transformation you create?

2. What systems or structures could you build to make your work more sustainable and scalable?

3. In what ways can you align purpose and profitability so that your impact grows without burnout?

4. Who around you is ready to rise into leadership — and are you creating the space for them to do it?

Growth requires courage — the courage to believe that integrity and abundance can coexist. Scaling with purpose isn't about building a bigger business; it's about building a stronger foundation.

9 HARD LESSONS

After building momentum with our adult programs, I began to think about the next generation — children and teens. I wanted to bring the same nutrition and lifestyle medicine principles that had changed the lives of so many adults into a program tailored for families. There was another dietitian who worked for me who had been hinting at wanting some ownership in the company more than once. I knew that intuitively that wasn't the right move to make, but I did offer to start a second company with her — a partnership — that would focus on the pediatric population.

That's how HINT RD — was born.

I made it clear. This new partnership *cannot take away* from RINT or *compete* with it. But, they can be two separate businesses that can co-exist and RINT can support HINT financially until it gets off the ground. I was willing to offer the resources with our EHR, office space, etc. I even invested my own money for the first few months to pay for our first pediatric dietitian.

I met another mom at my son's wrestling tournament and found out she was a pediatrician and owned her own practice.

"I think our new business can help your providers and patients. What do you think?" I asked her between our sons' matches.

We set up our first pediatric satellite location in northern Rhode Island at her women-owned pediatric practice. We signed the contract, set up the office — and referral system — in under a month.

It felt like a natural extension of what we were already doing — prevention, empowerment, and lifestyle change — but for the next generation.

For a while, it worked beautifully. HINT RD began attracting families across Rhode Island. We worked with pediatricians and community partners to support their patients and parents. We focused on nutrition for spectrum disorders, eating disorders, pediatric weight management, body positivity, and emotional well-being. It was deeply rewarding to help children and teens.

But as the program grew, something began to shift.
Our visions started to diverge.

What began as a shared mission slowly became misaligned in direction and values. Boundaries were blurred. I started noticing that some of RINT's adult patients were being redirected into the pediatric business — without transparency or agreement.

Then, one day, Kristin texted me:

"Did you agree to a $10 an hour raise and ten more hours per week for [your partner]? I just double checked your payroll and last month she gave herself a *big* pay raise."

I felt like I had been punched in the stomach. I wasn't taking a dime from the new business. I was giving money every week to help get it off the ground.

And when confronted, it was obvious that we had two very different perspectives when it came to leading with integrity. There was defensiveness and entitlement in every word spoken. She felt justified in stealing from the company, from stealing from me.

It was heartbreaking.

HINT RD was dissolved within two weeks. This was one of the hardest professional experiences I had faced. It wasn't just a financial drain, but also an emotional one. Not only was the business relationship over — the personal one was also over. It was like going through another divorce. A much smaller one, though — and without kids.

Lessons in Leadership and Integrity

That season taught me a valuable lesson of my career:

I learned that contracts and policies are not about mistrust — they're about protection and clearly communicating expectations. I learned that leadership isn't only about growth — it's also about how to navigate hard turns and come out stronger on the other side. And sometimes this means learning how to protect yourself, how to realign, and how to let go.

That experience made me a stronger businesswoman and a more grounded leader. It pushed me to fortify the systems and agreements at Rhode Island Nutrition Therapy, ensuring that as we continue to grow, we keep integrity, honesty and respect at it's core.

That also means that anything that disrupts our culture, has no place here.

Finding Purpose in the Pain — Again

Looking back, I see that chapter not as a failure, but as a refining moment — one that strengthened the integrity of everything that came after.

It reminded me that there are risks not just with starting a business, but also with growing it. There will always be more challenges. But the alternative — not taking risks, not facing new challenges, not finding out how you navigate your way when life gets tough — costs even more.

Side note: I had moments where I did look at this experience as a failure on my part. A failure to listen to my intuition. A failure to acknowledge the red flags that were waving at me along the way — warning me of what was to come.

However, I had to frame this as I would any other painful experience: another lesson intended for my growth. Every challenge along the way, especially the painful ones, has become the foundation for something greater.

HINT was a lesson in alignment — and it set the stage for the next phase of my journey.

REFLECTION

This chapter was about learning the hard way that leadership isn't just about vision — it's about values. Growth means nothing if integrity isn't at the center of it. Partnerships, like businesses, thrive only when trust, transparency, and alignment are non-negotiable.

Take a moment to reflect on your own leadership journey:

1. Have you ever ignored your intuition in a professional relationship? What did it cost you? In a personal relationship?

2. When you enter into partnerships or collaborations, how do you define and communicate boundaries?

3. Do you have systems and agreements in place that protect your time, energy, and integrity?

4. How do you respond when someone violates your trust or misaligns with your values — do you confront, correct, or let go?

5. In what ways can you strengthen your leadership so that generosity never comes at the expense of accountability?

Every business owner will face moments that test their ethics and resilience. These moments don't define failure — they define refinement. Integrity isn't a shield that prevents pain; it's the compass that keeps you moving in the right direction when things fall apart.

10 STAYING AWAKE

One day, I was scrolling through LinkedIn when an ad caught my eye — A company called Berry Street was hiring multiple contracted dietitians across the country. Curious, I clicked on their profile and noticed several other postings for positions at their headquarters in New York City.

The listings sounded more like an ad for a luxury vacation:

"Spacious and light-drenched 5,000-square-foot Madison Square Park office. All the seltzer and healthy snacks you could ask for."

A 5,000-square-foot Madison Square Park office?!

I was struggling to pay rent on three tiny office spaces — none of them sun-drenched and — overlooking parking lots. Out of curiosity, I looked up how much a 5,000-square-foot office in that area would cost. *$31,000 per month — and that was on the low end.*

But wait! There was more…

"Generous PTO. Comprehensive health insurance, including dental and vision. 401(k) with match. CitiBike membership for your NYC commute. Unlimited *dietitian* care. Competitive salary. Fast-scaling environment where you can take strong ownership."

But what really stood out to me was that those perks weren't being offered to the contracted dietitians. They were reserved for the "Associates".

Soon after, I saw another ad — this one from Fay. Then another, from Nourish. All of them were advertising national insurance-covered telehealth services, promising to "revolutionize nutrition care." When I dug deeper, I discovered that Nourish had raised an astonishing one billion dollars in venture capital to do just that.

But as I looked closer, I began to see cracks — serious ones.

The Bubble That's Already Forming

The explosion of telenutrition platforms might look like innovation, but it's actually market saturation disguised as progress. Each new company is promising the same thing — scale, access, disruption — while burning through massive amounts of investor capital to acquire patients they can't afford to keep. It's a race to the bottom built on unsustainable margins and unrealistic growth expectations.

The truth is, these platforms aren't revolutionizing nutrition care — they're commoditizing it. And like every overfunded health-tech wave before them, most won't survive once the venture capital dries up. When patient acquisition costs climb, investor patience runs out, and the reimbursement realities of healthcare set in, many of these companies will collapse under their own weight.

But that collapse also presents a massive opportunity.

When dietitians take ownership — building practices we *control*, where we own both the *patient and financial pipeline* — we create something far more durable than a startup built on subsidies. We can design systems that are ethical, compliant, and profitable — without answering to investors or algorithms. Ownership means stability. It means the power to decide how care is delivered, priced, and scaled. It's how we reclaim not just our profession, but the integrity and sustainability of nutrition care itself.

The Illusion of Scale

Telehealth startups are changing the landscape of dietetics — but not necessarily for the better. Backed by tens of millions in private equity, they promise nationwide access, streamlined systems, and "freedom" for dietitians through contracting. But behind the glossy marketing, the math often doesn't add up. These companies are spending tens of thousands of dollars a month on rent, technology, and administrative overhead, while relying on a network of more than a thousand dietitians classified as "independent contractors." Those dietitians are often told how long to meet with patients, what software to use, and how to document — all clear classification of an *employee*, not a *contractor.* It's a structure that allows corporations to skirt employee and employer taxes, benefits, and labor protections, while pushing the financial risk downstream to the very professionals generating their revenue.

The result is a fragile business model built on *borrowed* money and credibility. Private equity investors expect fast returns — not slow, steady growth. They demand higher margins, which means cutting corners wherever possible: lowering provider pay, automating care, and maximizing throughout. The problem is, you can't scale authentic care like an app. The pressure to serve investors instead of patients or providers — corrodes the mission of healthcare itself. Meanwhile, compliant small practices — those hiring dietitians as true employees, paying taxes, and following the rules — are forced to compete on an uneven playing field. This is the quiet crisis in our profession: the commercialization of nutrition care, driven not by values, but by venture capital's hunger for rapid growth and large investment returns.

Crossing the Line

These companies are growing fast, but not all are operating within the same ethical or legal standards that licensed professionals are held to. Some are violating state licensure laws, allowing dietitians to see patients across state lines without the required state license.

"They sent me patients from almost every state, even though I was licensed only in Rhode Island. I guess it's okay if they're doing it," a dietitian said in a sheepish tone as she shared her experience working for Nourish last year.

Others like Malla.co, were labeling registered dietitians as "health coaches" to bypass licensure requirements altogether — a direct violation of our Academy's Code of Ethics.

The more I researched, the more I realized how widespread it was.

Here we are, as registered dietitians, spending years earning degrees, completing supervised practice, passing national board exams, and maintaining continuing education, in order to protect the public and provide evidence-based care. Meanwhile, some of these new players were sidestepping those standards altogether, prioritizing growth and profit over ethics and safety.

In the end, it isn't the big tech companies who are liable for violating state licensure laws or our academy's code of ethics, it is the *registered dietitian* who will be held accountable. And that means every one of these dietitians is at risk of losing their license to practice *forever*. That means everything they have invested into their careers up until this point, all of the time and money spent on school, continuing education, etc. — to get them where they are today as a dietitian — can be taken away at the drop of a hat.

I was angry. It felt unfair that those of us doing things the right way were often the ones struggling to keep up financially — while companies cutting corners were being rewarded with massive valuations.

If these companies were going to redefine the nutrition landscape, then it was up to us — the credentialed, ethical, evidence-based professionals — to show what the future of nutrition care should really look like.

We could offer everything they promised — accessibility, innovation, scalability — but without compromising our integrity or violating laws designed to protect patients.

The Dietitian Revolution isn't just about helping dietitians make more money or grow their practices. It was about taking ownership, preserving the integrity of our profession and elevating it to its rightful place in healthcare.

The Startup Playbook

Venture capital firms don't invest to improve healthcare. They invest for one reason: massive returns.

The formula is always the same. First, they raise enormous amounts of money to build sleek telehealth platforms. Then they scale rapidly, adding thousands of patients and hundreds of dietitians as quickly as possible. Speed becomes more important than depth. Once they control the provider to patient pipeline, they start taking more control over how and what the provider is paid. Then, after consolidating the market, they sell to private equity or go public — and the clinical decision making and payment reimbursement models move even further away from the clinicians.

For startups, dietitians aren't viewed as healthcare providers. We're treated as labor units in a scaling equation. And for patients, that means care gets standardized, not specialized.

The Private Equity Problem

This isn't just about tech; it's about consolidation — and we've seen it happen before. In medicine, more than 75 percent of physicians are now employed by hospitals, health systems, or corporate medical groups. In dentistry, one in five practices is now owned by private equity-backed organizations that impose production quotas and cut appointment times to maximize profits. In mental health, online platforms like Talkspace and Betterhelp dominate the industry, turning providers into gig workers.

Dietitians are entering the same cycle. The rapid growth of telenutrition startups is only step one in a larger shift that will leave independent dietitians struggling to compete.

Why Dietitians Must Pay Attention

This isn't a distant threat; it's already here. Startups are securing exclusive payer contracts, limiting reimbursement options for independent practices. And as these companies grow, their goal is to increasingly absorb smaller practices — not to elevate them, but to control where the patients — and the money — goes.

If we don't innovate now, the decision about the future of dietetics won't be ours to make. It will be made for us — by venture capitalists, insurers, and private equity executives.

It Begins with Us

The truth is, dietitians don't need billion-dollar investors to validate the value of our work — we need each other. The real revolution begins when we reclaim our profession from the financial forces trying to reshape it. It starts in small, ethical practices that treat dietitians as professionals, not profit centers; that build sustainable models based on integrity, collaboration, and outcomes, not exploitation.

When we choose compliance over shortcuts, patient care over productivity quotas, and authenticity over automation, we're not just protecting our licenses — we're redefining what healthcare looks like. This is the movement that will outlast the venture-backed hype: a profession led by purpose, not profit.

The startups aren't slowing down. Private equity isn't backing off. Insurance companies are already choosing sides.

The question is this: will we lead the future of preventative medicine, or will we allow someone else to define it for us?

REFLECTION

This chapter was meant to be a wake-up call. Venture-backed startups and private equity aren't just reshaping healthcare — they're reshaping the role of dietitians. But disruption doesn't have to mean defeat. It can be the catalyst for redefining what's possible.

Take a moment to reflect on your place in this changing landscape:

1. How do you feel about the rise of venture-backed telehealth companies? Do you see them as partners, competitors, or something in between?

2. In your current role, how much control do you have over the way you practice? What would you change if you had full autonomy?

3. Where do you believe dietitians add value that technology and standardized protocols can't replace?

4. Are you prepared to innovate — to rethink your patient journey, adopt hybrid care models, or build collaborations — to stay competitive in the evolving healthcare ecosystem?

5. If we, as dietitians, don't lead the integration of personalized, preventative care into the future of healthcare, who will?

This isn't just about keeping up. It's about stepping up. The future of dietetics isn't being written by investors — unless we let it.

11 A NEW STANDARD OF CARE

In traditional healthcare, patients are often treated like problems to be solved rather than people to be understood. We set out to redefine that entirely — to establish a new standard of care grounded in connection, data, and dignity.

Our approach starts with listening. Every patient begins their journey with a 90-minute comprehensive assessment where we look at the whole person — not just their diet, but also their medical history, labs, medications, sleep, stress, environment, metabolic health, and readiness to change.

From there, we co-create a personalized care plan that addresses the entire person, not just a diagnosis. This single shift — seeing patients as human beings, not checklists — became the foundation of our success.

Building Our Hybrid Model of Care

From the start, we made a deliberate choice to create the best model of care for our patients. Our standard of care combines the best of both worlds: one-on-one Medical Nutrition Therapy (MNT) paired with group MNT programs designed to provide education, accountability, and peer support.

This hybrid approach has transformed how we deliver care. One-on-one sessions allow us to create individualized plans, while group programs give patients a sense of community and ongoing reinforcement between visits. Our group sessions are designed around the science of behavior change — building skills, confidence, and lifelong habits rather than simply handing out information.

And patients don't feel alone. They are with others on a similar journey. There is power in the group.

Patients love it. Dietitians love it. And the outcomes prove that it works.

But what makes this model truly revolutionary isn't just its structure — it's ownership. We control every step of the patient and financial pipeline, ensuring care decisions are made by clinicians, not corporations. That's how quality stays high, compliance stays intact, and sustainability becomes possible.

Partnering for Prevention

As we grew, our impact extended beyond the walls of our practice. We partnered with the Rhode Island Department of Health (RIDOH) and the CDC to integrate the Prevent T2 program into our services — a 12-month, evidence-based lifestyle change program designed to reverse prediabetes and prevent type 2 diabetes.

But there's a problem with how this program is structured nationally. The CDC requires only a lifestyle coach to lead the Prevent T2 program, despite the fact that its entire curriculum focuses on reversing a disease — prediabetes. In most states, this violates dietetics licensure laws and puts vulnerable populations at risk of receiving misguided nutrition information from individuals who may not be adequately trained.

At our practice, the Prevent T2 program is dietitian-led, with lifestyle coaches supporting rather than replacing the expertise of registered dietitians. Patients deserve evidence-based care — especially when the stakes are as high as preventing diabetes.

This is what prevention looks like when it's done right — not a volume game, but a value game. Prevention should never be commoditized; it should be clinically led, data-informed, and ethically delivered.

The Fight for Fair Coverage

Our model works. But the healthcare system hasn't caught up.

Dietitians are still underutilized, underpaid, and undervalued compared to other healthcare providers — even as the evidence mounts that we are uniquely positioned to prevent and reverse chronic disease. Despite better outcomes and lower long-term costs, coverage for dietitian-led care remains limited, especially in preventative services.

We need systemic change. We need expanded reimbursement for services like Remote Therapeutic Monitoring (RTM) and Remote Patient Monitoring (RPM), which allow dietitians to track patient progress and intervene between appointments before complications arise. We need coverage for collaboration with referring physicians and specialists, because coordinated care leads to better outcomes. And we need Medicare and Medicaid reimbursement for preventative services, particularly for conditions like heart disease, obesity, and prediabetes, where early intervention can save lives and reduce costs.

Right now, the lack of access isn't just a policy gap — it's a healthcare disparity. And it's one we intend to close — not by waiting for policy to catch up, but by proving what's possible when dietitians take the lead.

Proving It Works

The results speak for themselves. Patients in our hybrid programs lose, on average, eight to twelve percent of their body weight within 12 weeks. Among those who fully engage with their care plan, we've seen prediabetes reversal rates as high as sixty percent. We've helped patients lower blood pressure, improve lab markers, reduce medication use under physician supervision, and, most importantly, gain control over their health.

We share this data with our referring physicians, insurers, and the CDC — because data speak louder than marketing budgets. Our numbers don't just validate our model — they redefine what success in healthcare can look like when care is clinician-led, not investor-driven.

The Bigger Picture

This model isn't just about our practice; it's about proving something bigger.

Dietitians don't have to sell out to survive. We don't have to choose between independence and innovation.

We can design care models that compete — and win — on our own terms. By centering care around patients, outcomes, and connection, we've created something private equity can't touch and algorithms can't replace.

At RINT, our mission isn't just to change how nutrition care is delivered — it's to redefine who controls it. The future of healthcare belongs to the providers who build it with integrity.

But the truth is, we can't do this alone. We need stronger advocacy. We need policy reform. And we need to unify as a profession to protect our role in shaping the future of healthcare.

Because if we don't lead, someone else will. And if we allow that to happen, our value — and our patients' outcomes — will continue to be defined by people who have never sat across from a patient, heard their fears, or walked them through change one step at a time.

REFLECTION

This chapter paints a vision for the future of dietetics — one where dietitians lead prevention, innovation, and patient-centered care. Take a moment to connect this to your own role in shaping what comes next.

1. When you think about the model described in this chapter — combining 1:1 MNT, group MNT, and collaboration with broader healthcare teams — where do you see yourself fitting in?

2. How do you feel about lifestyle-change programs like Prevent T2 being led by non-dietitians? What responsibility do you think we have to advocate for evidence-based care in these spaces?

3. If expanded coverage and reimbursement became a reality — for RTM, RPM, and preventative services — how would that change the way you practice, the patients you serve, or the programs you offer?

Explore how your personal goals align with the future of our profession — and where you want to lead from here.

12 FROM FEAR TO FUEL

I had reached a point in my career and life where I realized something powerful:

I am 100% capable of taking care of my children on my own.

For years, child support had been a part of my financial stability after my divorce. It was there to help with the kids' needs, and I was grateful for it. But as time went on, something in my spirit began to stir.

I felt God was asking me to take a new step — *a faith step.*

So I did something a little unusual. I told my ex-husband to stop paying child support.

When I told close friends, they looked at me in disbelief. When I told my lawyer, he shook his head.

"Why would you do that?" "Child support is for the children, not for you."

And they were right — child support *is* for the children. But my decision wasn't about money; it was about pushing myself to a new level.

I knew that removing that safety net would push me to think differently — to make decisions differently. When things are comfortable, it's easy to coast. But when there's pressure, you get creative. You take risks. You stretch yourself beyond what feels safe.

If I saw less money in the bank, I didn't panic — I innovated. Okay, let me be truly honest here: *I did panic.* But only at first. Then, I turned that fear into the fuel I needed to think differently. It made me sharper, more focused, more creative.

This was my way of stepping fully into the belief that dietitians — and *women* — are capable of building wealth, independence, and legacy on their own terms.

I wanted to model that strength for my children: the strength that comes from faith, courage, and an unshakable belief in your own ability to create something meaningful.

Letting go of child support wasn't about proving something to anyone else — it was about proving something to *myself*.

It was about standing in full ownership of my life, my purpose, and my path.

Child support had kept me dependent on a man who I had worked hard to separate from — and it gave him the sense that he still had some control over me.

So, I let it go.

And with that new challenge, I was now rooted even deeper in faith and resilience.

There is always risk when we decide to discover what we are capable of — but the reward is always be greater.

The Next Level: Thinking Bigger

When I removed that safety net, something shifted in me. It pushed me to ask bigger questions:

How can I take the business to a new level?
How can I use what we've already built to change the trajectory?

For years, we had been quietly developing something powerful — our group programs. Programs like Prevent T2, Total Lifestyle Change (TLC), Nutrition Academy, and Metabolic Weight Management had become the backbone of our practice.

We had tested, refined, and proven that these programs worked — not just clinically, but financially. They provided structure, accountability, and measurable outcomes for patients, while giving dietitians a way to serve more people efficiently.

And that's when the idea hit me:

What if our next level of growth isn't just Business to Consumer (B2C) — what if it's Business to Business (B2B)?

We could help other dietitians grow by sharing the very systems, frameworks, and programs we had been building since 2020.

Because the truth is, dietitians can no longer sustain their businesses solely on 1:1 Medical Nutrition Therapy. The math doesn't work. Reimbursement rates remain low, and there are only so many hours in a day. This model only leads to burnout.

The only way to grow — the only way to make a lasting impact and earn what we're worth — is to scale differently. For us, that meant group programs.

Group programs allow you to reach more patients, diversify income, and create deeper transformation through community support. They also make healthcare more accessible and affordable — bridging the gap between personalized care and scalable impact.

I realized that the next level for us wasn't just about serving more patients. It was about empowering more providers.

Our programs had become a blueprint — not just for nutrition care, but for business sustainability.

If we could teach other dietitians how to implement them, integrate them with their EHRs, and build collaborative relationships with physicians, we could multiply our impact exponentially.

Instead of selling directly to patients, we could license our programs and systems to other private practices, hospitals, or community health organizations. These programs could be white-labeled, customized with their logos, and integrated into their workflows.

Our mission expanded once again:

To empower dietitians across the country to scale ethically, profitably, and sustainably — while transforming the health of their communities.

While tech companies were cutting corners and bypassing licensure laws, we were offering a compliant, evidence-based alternative — one built *by* dietitians, *for* dietitians.

Creating the Licensing Framework

The first step was to turn our group programs into licensable assets. We began developing a framework that would allow other dietitians and healthcare practices to license our programs under their own brands.

Each program — like Prevent T2, TLC, Nutrition Academy, and Metabolic Weight Management — would be fully integrated into the EHR, complete with:

- Facilitator guides and session outlines

- Editable marketing templates

- Outcome tracking forms

- Customizable branding (so practices could white-label them with their own logos)

- Built-in compliance and documentation tools aligned with payer requirements

The goal was to make it plug-and-play — so any practice could launch a lifestyle medicine group within weeks, not months.

We weren't just offering a product. We were offering a blueprint.

Partnering with Healthie

To make this possible, we deepened our partnership with Healthie, our EHR and practice management platform.

Healthie became the foundation for how these programs would be delivered, tracked, and scaled. We worked on developing the systems for group scheduling, secure messaging, outcomes reporting, and billing integration — all within one seamless environment.

Through Healthie's shared program feature, practices could use our programs under their own name, within their own Healthie account, while maintaining consistency and data integrity across sites.

It was the perfect marriage of information and technology — blending modern efficiency with evidence-based care.

Developing Training and Support

Next came training. I knew that if we wanted these programs to succeed beyond our walls, we couldn't just hand over materials — we had to teach the mindset and model behind them.

So we began developing training modules and onboarding resources for partner dietitians. These covered everything from:

- How to funnel 1:1 patients into group MNT programs

- How to market groups to physicians and to the community

- How to track and report outcomes

- How to align with payer policies and HIPAA compliance

- How to lead with compassion, confidence, and clinical excellence

This was about more than business — it was about empowerment.

We were equipping dietitians to think like leaders, not just clinicians.

The Bigger Vision

As I built this framework, I began to see the ripple effect more clearly than ever.

Each practice that would adopt one of our programs wasn't just adding revenue — they were expanding access to care, strengthening physician partnerships, and elevating the role of dietitians in healthcare.

We were no longer building one practice.
We were building an ecosystem — a nationwide network of registered

dietitians and healthcare professionals working collaboratively under one shared mission:

To make nutrition and lifestyle medicine the foundation of preventive care.

And for the first time, I could see the full picture:

The systems we had spent years creating were now ready to empower others.

What began as one practice in Rhode Island had become the foundation for something far greater — a movement to redefine how healthcare is delivered and how dietitians thrive within it.

REFLECTION

Before moving forward, take a moment to reflect on what this chapter truly represents — the courage to release what feels safe in order to reach what feels possible.
Faith steps are rarely logical. They ask us to trust in something unseen — our purpose, our potential, our ability to create more than we've ever known.

Let these questions help you explore your own leaps of faith and growth:

1. What "safety nets" in your life or business have you been holding onto? What would happen if you loosened your grip and trusted yourself — or God — to fill the gap?

2. When have you taken a leap of faith that changed how you saw yourself? How did that decision stretch your capacity and expand your courage?

3. Where in your work are you still thinking like a provider instead of a builder? What might change if you began designing systems that create freedom, not just stability?

4. What gifts or frameworks have you developed that could empower others? How could sharing your hard-earned lessons multiply your impact?

5. How do you define abundance — and how does faith influence that definition? What would it look like to believe that doing good and thriving financially are not opposites, but partners

6. Who might be waiting for you to take your next faith step — to model courage, independence, and purpose for them, as you did for your children?

Write down the answers that surface — or simply sit with them in silence.
Faith often whispers before it shouts. Trust the whisper.
You may already be standing at the edge of your next big leap — the one that leads to growth, freedom, and a ripple of impact beyond anything you can yet see.

13 SCALING OUT — NOT SELLING OUT

Before we can build models that thrive, we have to understand what sets us apart. Dietitians bring something to healthcare that no algorithm, tech startup, or even physician can replicate: we personalize care at the deepest level, meeting patients where they are and tailoring strategies to their unique biology, preferences, and lifestyles. We lead with prevention, helping people reduce risk and reverse disease before it becomes pathology. We know how to build habits that last, guiding real, sustainable behavior change instead of handing over quick-fix meal plans. And we see the whole person, not just the lab results or diagnosis, treating the human in front of us rather than a checklist.

Starting Small, Building Smart

You don't need a ten-person team, a massive infrastructure, or a multi-program model to innovate. You can begin exactly where you are. Redesigning the patient journey starts with creating a clear and consistent process from intake to maintenance, focusing on outcomes rather than visit counts. We've done this by integrating our hybrid model of care — combining personalized one-on-one sessions with small group medical nutrition therapy programs that scale our time without sacrificing quality.

Patients benefit from individualized plans and ongoing community-based support, and our dietitians thrive because they can deliver high-touch care while serving more people. We also leverage technology intentionally — using secure telehealth platforms, patient messaging, and even wearables to enhance connection, not replace it. From day one, we started tracking outcomes, even when we only had a handful of patients. Those early numbers became the foundation of everything that came next.

Using Data as Leverage

Data changes the conversation. Big platforms win payer contracts because they promise outcomes, but we can prove them. By tracking metrics like weight reduction, reversal of prediabetes and metabolic syndrome, improvements in labs and blood pressure, reductions in medication use, and patient engagement rates, we build undeniable evidence of impact.

In our practice, sharing this data with referring physicians, insurers, and employers transformed how we were seen. We stopped asking for credibility and started commanding it. Suddenly, conversations shifted from "why should we refer to you?" to "how can we partner with you?"

Reimagining Revenue Models

One of the biggest mistakes private practices make is relying exclusively on MNT billing. It creates a fragile business model and limits our ability to innovate. We've expanded our approach by integrating multiple revenue streams while keeping patients at the center of care. Insurance-based services remain foundational, but we've added group programs, testing packages, supplement pathways, and employer contracts for corporate wellness and prevention programs.

For patients who want additional support, we offer out-of-pocket options and models that provide ongoing access to testing, follow-ups, and digital tracking. These diversified revenue streams make our practice more resilient while preserving autonomy — and, most importantly, they allow us to reinvest in delivering better care.

Building a Brand That Patients Trust

Startups win attention because they have marketing budgets. Dietitians win loyalty by earning trust.

We've focused on sharing real patient success stories, educating our community about preventive medicine, and positioning ourselves as thought leaders in nutrition and lifestyle care. By publishing outcomes, speaking at conferences, and contributing to professional conversations, we've built a brand grounded in authenticity, not advertising. That trust has scaled further than any paid campaign ever could.

Thinking Bigger Than Your Practice

This is about more than growing individual businesses. It's about changing the trajectory of our profession.

Imagine thousands of dietitians across the country delivering high-touch, data-driven hybrid care models within their communities. Imagine us collectively demonstrating outcomes strong enough to influence insurers, policymakers, and healthcare systems. Imagine reclaiming our role as leaders in preventative medicine — not as optional support, but as essential providers at the center of chronic disease care.

This isn't a pipe dream. It's already happening. But it starts with a choice: we can keep doing business the same way until decisions are made for us, or we can innovate now, protect our autonomy, and build a future where dietitians lead the preventative medicine revolution.

In the next chapter, we'll explore how we unify as a profession — advocating for stronger reimbursement, protecting our scope, and ensuring that our voices shape the future of nutrition care, not just venture capitalists and insurance executives.

REFLECTION

This chapter challenges you to think differently about your role — not just as a provider, but as a leader shaping the future of our profession. Before moving on, take a moment to reflect on where you stand and where you want to go.

1.   What sets you apart as a dietitian — the one thing you do differently from any algorithm, app, or protocol?

2.   How are you currently tracking patient outcomes, and how could data become your leverage to build credibility, partnerships, and influence?

3.   What opportunities exist in your community — with physicians, hospitals, employers, or public health programs — that could help you expand your impact?

Explore your ideas, challenge old assumptions, and imagine the bigger role you could play in shaping the future of dietetics.

14 FUTURE-PROOFING DIETETICS

A few months ago, a new patient said something that stopped me cold.

"I talked to this new AI nutrition app before this appointment," she told me. "It told me exactly what to eat to reverse my prediabetes. Do I even need a dietitian?"

That question shook me — not because I doubted my value, but because I realized just how quickly the landscape of nutrition care is shifting.

AI is here. Digital health platforms are everywhere. And patients are starting to wonder if they still need us.

But here's the truth: technology isn't the enemy. The real danger lies in losing the human connection.

The Rise of AI-Driven Nutrition Care

Tech startups like Nourish, Faye, and Berry Street are racing to integrate AI into their platforms. Their goals are simple: automate patient education, standardize care protocols, and optimize patient pathways using predictive analytics — all designed to scale faster and reach more people.

And now, there's a new shift underway. Noom may become the first telehealth platform to offer an asynchronous diabetes prevention lifestyle change program that includes nutrition advice for people with prediabetes and other metabolic conditions. Even more concerning, their next step is positioning themselves to submit for insurance reimbursement — based primarily on AI-driven recommendations, not clinician-led care.

At first glance, this sounds like progress: more access, more convenience, more reach. But efficiency comes at a cost. Protocol-driven care leaves little room for personalization. AI-generated recommendations lack context and nuance. And while these tools deliver information, they rarely drive lasting transformation.

The truth is, patients love the convenience. They like instant answers and simple plans. And if we, as dietitians, ignore AI and digital tools entirely, we risk becoming invisible — to consumers, insurers, and healthcare systems alike.

What Technology Can't Replace

AI can process data faster than we ever could. It can generate meal plans, analyze lab results, and make generalized recommendations. But it can't sit with a patient while they cry over a lifetime of failed diets. It can't celebrate the five-pound weight loss that represents years of regained hope. It can't consider the trauma, culture, family dynamics, and deeply personal relationships people have with food.

It also can't coach someone through the messy, nonlinear process of behavior change. That's where dietitians shine. Technology can provide information. Dietitians provide connection, context, and transformation.

That's where we win — if we're willing to evolve.

Using Technology to Enhance, Not Replace, Care

The mistake many startups make is assuming technology should replace human care. The real opportunity lies in using tech to amplify what makes dietitians irreplaceable: personalization and partnership.

In our practice, we've integrated technology intentionally — on our terms. We use Healthie's AI Scribe to support more efficient and consistent charting by our dietitians. This allows us to turn progress notes around quickly and provide referring providers with a standardized, concise summary of their patient's progress.

We call this our VIP Provider Program, and providers are thrilled to receive communication from us. They're simply not used to hearing back from the dietitians they refer their patients to. This has also become one of our most effective ways to market to providers. A patient may come to us on their own, without a referral, and when their provider receives our progress notes and follows up with their patient, we — as dietitians — are now top of mind for the next individual who needs nutrition and lifestyle intervention.

We've also incorporated data tracking into our model by integrating wearables such as continuous glucose monitors, Apple Watches, Bluetooth scales, and blood pressure cuffs. Many of these devices automatically collect and upload real-time patient data into the patient portal. At each follow-up session, we review this information with the patient, interpret it clinically, and translate it into realistic action steps that become part of their wellness plan.

Through remote therapeutic monitoring, patients share personal wins, struggles, and patterns between appointments, allowing us to address their needs proactively.

We also use secure messaging and engagement tools in Healthie to help patients stay motivated and accountable between visits, sending personalized reminders and tailored nudges to keep patients motivated. Our outcome dashboards help patients visualize progress, making the impact of their choices visible and real.

The goal isn't to replace dietitians with dashboards or algorithms. It's to enhance our effectiveness while keeping human connection at the center of care.

Becoming the Interpreter, Not the Replaced

As AI tools generate more reports, predictive scores, and automated nutrition plans, patients will increasingly come to us with recommendations already in hand — from apps, wearables, and digital platforms. Our role is shifting from being the sole source of information to being the interpreter of information.

Patients need us to translate data into actionable strategies that make sense for their unique circumstances. We help them navigate conflicting recommendations, choose the right priorities, and take steps that actually work for their bodies and their lives.

In a world drowning in data, the value of dietitians isn't shrinking. It's growing.

Leading the Digital Integration Movement

But we need to act — fast. If dietitians don't lead the conversation around digital integration, startups and insurers will define it for us. They will decide how nutrition care is delivered, which tech platforms are approved, and how reimbursement gets structured. Noom's shift toward asynchronous, AI-driven prevention programs is just the beginning.

The future of dietetics is not algorithm-driven — it's human-driven, supported by technology. AI can summarize research, but it can't sit in silence when a patient shares their shame around food. It can't foster trust. It can't tailor solutions around culture, traditions, and identity. And it can't be a partner in lasting lifestyle change.

Patients don't stay engaged with apps because of features. They stay engaged because someone believes in them. That belief — that partnership — is our competitive edge.

Future-Proofing the Profession

To thrive in a tech-driven world, we must embrace technology strategically while doubling down on the human connection that makes dietitians essential. That means integrating tools like wearables, telehealth, and data dashboards without letting them replace personalization. It means tracking outcomes rigorously to prove our value to payers, providers, and employers. And it means advocating for stronger reimbursement protections so insurance doesn't default to funding AI-driven platforms over dietitian-led care.

We also need to educate physicians, insurers, and policymakers about the risks of allowing asynchronous AI-driven nutrition programs to replace evidence-based, patient-centered care. As Noom and similar platforms move toward insurance reimbursement, it's critical we make the case for dietitian-led models that blend technology and human expertise responsibly.

Looking Ahead

AI and digital health aren't going away. The question isn't whether they'll reshape dietetics — it's how.

We can either let startups and insurers define our role, or we can lead the integration of technology into nutrition care on our terms.

This isn't just about adapting to change. It's about protecting the future of our profession and ensuring patients receive safe, effective, and personalized care.

REFLECTION

Technology is reshaping healthcare — and dietetics is at the center of it. This reflection invites you to consider how you'll adapt, lead, and protect your value as a clinician in a digital-first world.

1. How does the rise of AI-driven platforms like Noom, Nourish, and Berry Street make you feel — excited, frustrated, threatened, or inspired? Why?

2. What aspects of your care cannot be replicated by an app, an algorithm, or a standardized protocol?

3. How comfortable are you with integrating technology like wearables, remote monitoring, or telehealth into your practice? Where could these tools enhance patient outcomes without replacing personalization?

4. If startups begin receiving reimbursement for asynchronous, AI-driven nutrition care, how will you position yourself — and your services — to remain indispensable?

Explore your beliefs, your value, and your vision for how dietitians can thrive in a tech-driven future.

15 RECLAIMING OUR FIELD

There's a hard truth we need to face: for too long, dietitians have been on the sidelines of healthcare.

We are clinically trained, licensed professionals with the power to reverse chronic disease, lower costs, and transform lives. Yet the healthcare system — and yes, even our own professional organizations — have failed to position us as essential providers. While we've been busy counseling patients, building practices, and doing the work we were trained to do, others have been writing the rules about how, where, and even if we get to practice.

Insurers decide how much our time is worth. Private equity decides how care is delivered. Startups decide how we show up in telehealth. Legislators decide our scope of practice — often without our voices in the room.

It's time to change that. It's time to advocate like our profession depends on it — because it does.

The Reimbursement Reality

Dietitians are chronically undervalued by insurers. In many states, we are still fighting for reimbursement parity — meaning we're either reimbursed at lower rates than other providers for delivering the exact same services or excluded from coverage entirely.

Meanwhile, startups like Nourish, Fay and Berry Street are negotiating exclusive payer contracts that effectively lock independent dietitians out of networks we've spent years building relationships with. This isn't accidental. It's leverage — and right now, we don't have enough of it.

To change this, we must lead with outcomes and unity. Data drives payer negotiations, and without it, we remain powerless. We need to track measurable patient outcomes — weight reductions, prediabetes reversal rates, reductions in medication use, improved labs — and use that data to demonstrate our value. We also need to join forces locally, forming state-level coalitions of private practice dietitians to negotiate as a collective rather than one by one. And we must engage directly with insurers and policymakers, educating them about the cost savings and improved outcomes that evidence-based, dietitian-led care delivers.

When we act together, we gain bargaining power. But if we stay fragmented, insurers will continue to decide our value without us at the table.

Closing the Leadership Gap

There's another difficult question we need to ask: where have our professional organizations been?

While private equity-backed telehealth companies consolidate power and venture-capital-funded startups control access to patients, our leadership bodies have been slow to respond. They've fought for recognition, yes — but recognition isn't the same as influence. They haven't built us leverage where we need it most.

That doesn't mean we give up on them. It means we step up around them. We need to form state-level advocacy groups that can act faster than national organizations, build alliances with physicians and nurse practitioners who understand the value of preventative medicine, and partner with patient advocacy groups that want nutrition at the center of healthcare reform.

If we wait for someone else to lead us, we'll always be reacting instead of shaping the future. And by then, it may be too late.

Pushing Back on Private Equity

What's happening in dietetics isn't new — we've already seen it in medicine, dentistry, and behavioral health. Private equity buys up practices, negotiates exclusive payer contracts, standardizes protocols to maximize throughput, and then sells the consolidated platform for billions. The clinicians — the ones driving patient care and outcomes — are left with less autonomy, more quotas, and lower pay.

We are next.

The only way to push back is to stay independent, innovate collectively, and demonstrate our value. That means forming regional RD networks to share resources, negotiate payer contracts together, and integrate collaborative care partnerships with physicians and NPs to strengthen our bargaining power. It also means leveraging outcomes-driven data to prove that independent dietitian-led care delivers better patient results and lower costs than commoditized care delivered by corporate platforms.

Private equity thrives when we stay fragmented. We win when we unify and differentiate ourselves.

Protecting Our Scope

If we don't actively defend our scope of practice, others will erode it — intentionally or simply because we're not in the room. Startups are hiring health coaches and uncertified nutritionists to deliver standardized protocols. Telehealth platforms are leaning on AI-driven recommendations instead of clinician-led care. Legislators, often without input from registered dietitians, are expanding access for non-credentialed providers to deliver "nutrition counseling."

Our response must be twofold. First, we need legislative advocacy at the state level to strengthen licensure laws and ensure that only qualified professionals deliver evidence-based care. Second, we need public education campaigns to help patients understand the difference between evidence-based medical nutrition therapy and general nutrition advice.

We can't assume patients — or policymakers — know the difference. We have to show them why we matter.

Policy Is Power

Change doesn't happen just in clinics or boardrooms — it happens in policy.

For too long, dietitians have been left out of the conversations that shape how we can practice, get reimbursed, and reach patients. That realization became personal for me the day I received a small postcard in the mail from the Rhode Island Academy of Nutrition and Dietetics. It announced that our state affiliate had hired a lobbyist to help pass legislation that would extend telehealth coverage for dietitians beyond the COVID-19 emergency.

At the time, telehealth had transformed access to care for so many of our patients. Rolling back that coverage would have meant forcing countless individuals — many managing chronic disease — to lose continuity of care simply because they couldn't make it into an office. That postcard was more than an update; it was a wake-up call.

Soon after, I joined the RIAND board. I wanted to be part of the work that ensures our voices are heard — not after decisions are made, but *before*.

The following year, I testified at the Rhode Island State House before both the House and Senate committees in support of the Dietitian Licensure Compact. I spoke about how expanding interstate licensure would protect patient access, streamline compliance, and give registered dietitians the ability to practice across state lines legally and ethically — while maintaining the integrity of our profession.

In 2024, Rhode Island became the fourteenth state to pass the Dietitian Licensure Compact bill. That moment was more than symbolic; it was proof that when dietitians show up, policy moves.

But this is just the beginning.
If we want to protect our scope of practice, secure fair coverage, and ensure ethical, evidence-based care remains in the hands of credentialed professionals, we must continue to advocate — relentlessly.

Policy isn't politics. It's the infrastructure of access — the framework that determines who gets care, how it's paid for, and who's allowed to provide it.
And if we don't lead those conversations, someone else will.

Dietitians belong at every table where healthcare decisions are made — from hospital systems to state legislatures. Because the future of nutrition care won't just be written in research journals or business plans; it will be written into law.

We can't afford to stay silent anymore. We need to call legislators and demand reimbursement parity, inclusion in value-based care models, and stronger licensure protections. We need to join coalitions where decisions are actually being made, educate physicians and employers about the cost savings of food-first care, and hold our professional organizations accountable for stronger, faster action.

Advocacy isn't optional anymore. It's survival.

The Crossroads We Face

We are at a turning point. If we stay quiet, startups, private equity firms, and insurers will decide the future of dietetics without us.
But if we innovate, unify, and advocate right now, we can reclaim our power, protect our autonomy, and position dietitians where we belong: at the forefront of the preventative medicine revolution.

REFLECTION

This chapter calls us to step off the sidelines and into leadership. Before moving forward, take a moment to reflect on your role in shaping the future of our profession.

1. Where do you see gaps in your state's policies, reimbursement models, or licensure protections that directly impact your ability to practice?

2. How are you currently tracking and sharing patient outcomes to demonstrate your value to insurers, physicians, or policymakers?

3. What steps could you take to get more involved in advocacy — whether at the local, state, or national level?

4. If dietitians unified and spoke with one voice, what could change for our profession, for patients, and for the healthcare system as a whole?

Identify where your influence begins — and where you're ready to step forward to protect, elevate, and transform the future of dietetics.

16 THE DIETITIAN REVOLUTION

There's a moment in every profession when everything changes.

For physicians, it was the rise of private equity and hospital consolidation. For therapists, it was the launch of mass-scale digital platforms like Talkspace and BetterHelp.

For dietitians, that moment is right now.

And we have a choice to make. We can allow startups, insurers, and investors to define who we are, what we do, and what we're worth. Or we can rise together, innovate boldly, and lead the preventative medicine revolution ourselves.

The Power of "We"

Individually, dietitians are strong advocates for our patients. But collectively, we are an untapped powerhouse — and the healthcare system knows it. There are over 100,000 registered dietitians in the U.S., working across every corner of care: hospitals, clinics, schools, private practice, public health, tech, and policy.

We are the only professionals clinically trained to deliver nutrition-based interventions proven to prevent, reverse, and manage chronic disease. And yet, we are still too often treated as optional support staff while less qualified providers — and even AI-driven apps — are elevated above us.

This isn't a competency problem. It's a power problem. And power comes from organization, influence, and outcomes.

Uniting Around a Shared Mission

If we want to lead the future, we have to define it.

Our shared mission is simple but bold: to position dietitians as the leaders of food-first, preventative medicine and reclaim our place as essential providers in an evolving healthcare system.

That requires a shift in how we see ourselves. We are not simply "nutrition educators." We are healthcare disruptors. We are not "adjunct providers." We are leaders in chronic disease prevention. And we are not isolated competitors fighting for referrals — we are collectives building ecosystems of care.

When we unify behind this identity, everything changes.

Building Regional RD Innovation Networks

Startups are winning right now because they've built centralized infrastructure. But we can replicate that power — without giving up our independence.

Imagine regional RD innovation networks in every state: independent dietitians collaborating instead of competing, sharing resources like EHR systems and tech platforms, pooling outcome data to create reports insurers can't ignore, and establishing referral pathways with physicians, nurse practitioners, and specialists to become the backbone of preventative care pipelines.

When one practice becomes part of a network, and networks connect across the country, we shift markets. Together, we can create a model of care that is stronger, smarter, and more patient-centered than anything startups can scale.

Influencing Policy, Together

If we want better reimbursement, stronger licensure laws, and protections against being replaced by unqualified providers or AI-driven apps, we must show up where decisions are made. Legislators respond to organized, outcome-driven voices — and for too long, we've been too quiet.

We need to demonstrate the value of dietitians in preventing and reversing chronic disease, sharing patient success stories alongside hard data. By doing this collectively, we create undeniable leverage. When we speak with one voice, policymakers will finally be forced to listen.

Owning the Public Narrative

We also need to control how patients see us. Right now, too many people don't understand the difference between a registered dietitian and a health coach — or an algorithm. That has to change.

It's time to launch a unified public narrative about who we are and why our work matters. Through national campaigns, digital media, podcasts, and storytelling, we need to educate patients about the unique value of evidence-based, dietitian-led care. When people understand the difference, they will choose us.

Leading the Technology Conversation

AI, wearables, and telehealth aren't going away. But we cannot afford to sit on the sidelines while tech startups redefine nutrition care without us. Instead of resisting innovation, we must lead it.

Dietitians should be setting the standards for data privacy, patient safety, and tech-integrated care. We need to collaborate with technology partners who elevate, rather than replace, our expertise. And we must educate insurers and employers on why dietitian-led, tech-enhanced models produce better outcomes than any algorithm or standardized protocol.

If we lead, we shape the rules. If we stay silent, we become the product.

Building the National Dietitian Collective

This is the bigger vision: a connected, national network of dietitians pooling outcomes, leveraging shared digital infrastructure, and negotiating collectively with insurers, employers, and tech platforms. A centralized advocacy voice that legislators and payers can't ignore. A public-facing brand that finally educates patients about why they need registered dietitians — and why no app or startup can replace us.

This isn't about replacing existing professional organizations. It's about moving faster than they can.

The Call to Lead

The disruption is here. Private equity is consolidating. Startups are scaling. Insurance companies are choosing sides. And technology is accelerating faster than policy can keep up.

But this is our profession. Our patients. Our future.

We can either allow others to decide what dietitians are worth, or we can define it for ourselves.

This is the Dietitian Revolution.
It starts with us.
It starts now.
And it starts together.

REFLECTION

This chapter is about collective power — the strength we hold when we unify, innovate, and lead. Take a moment to reflect on your role in shaping the future of our profession.

1.   How do you currently see your role as a registered dietitian — as an individual provider or as part of a larger movement?

2.   What does "leading the preventative medicine revolution" mean to you personally?

3.   If thousands of dietitians joined forces to build regional innovation networks and pool collective data, what would that make possible for patients, for our profession, and for healthcare?

4.   What first step could you take today to connect, collaborate, or contribute to a unified vision for dietitians?

The future of dietetics isn't being written for us — it's being written by us. This is your moment to claim your voice, your value, and your role in the revolution.

CONCLUSION: BECOME THE DISRUPTION

We are the generation of dietitians standing on a fault line. On one side is an outdated healthcare model that waits for disease to happen and treats symptoms after the fact. On the other is a wave of venture-capital-backed disruption threatening to commoditize preventative care and minimize our role.

But there is a third path — our path. We have the power to lead the change ourselves. That means innovating boldly in our practices, advocating fiercely for our profession, and uniting behind a shared mission of food-first, preventative medicine.

Because if we don't, we risk waking up one day to find our profession unrecognizable — not because we weren't needed, but because we didn't fight for our place.

The Revolution Starts Here

I didn't write this book to inspire you. I wrote it to activate you.

The future of dietetics doesn't belong to private equity firms, telehealth startups, or insurance companies. It belongs to us — but only if we take it. We are the innovators. We are the disruptors. We are the future of preventative medicine.

But a movement isn't built by one person, one practice, or even one book. It's built when thousands of us decide — together — that we will no longer wait for permission to lead.

This is the Dietitian Revolution. And it starts with you. Right now.

Your Next Chapter

This isn't the end of the book. It's the beginning of something bigger. Change starts with small, intentional actions. In your practice, rethink how patients experience care. Redesign your patient journey, track your outcomes, and integrate hybrid models that combine personalized one-on-one care with the power of group-based support. In your community, connect with other dietitians. Share resources, build local networks, and create stronger referral pipelines.

Within our profession, speak up. Advocate. Call your legislators. Join payer negotiation groups. Push for stronger licensure laws, better reimbursement, and parity with other providers. Make your voice impossible to ignore. And within the broader movement, tell your story. Share your wins. Let your success inspire others to step forward, too.

Together, we are redefining dietetics. Together, we are reclaiming preventative medicine. Together, we are unstoppable.

REFLECTION

This chapter is about choosing between standing on the sidelines or stepping into leadership. Take a moment to pause and reflect on where you are — and where you want to go.

1. What first inspired you to become a dietitian? Does that original "why" still guide you today?

2. When you think about the future of dietetics, what excites you — and what scares you the most?

3. Where do you feel you've been playing small in your career, and what would it look like to step into your full potential?

4. What's one action you can take this month — in your practice, your community, or the profession — to strengthen your voice and expand your impact?

7. How do you want to be remembered in this movement? As someone who watched change happen — or as someone who helped create it?

The Dietitian Revolution isn't a concept. It's a choice. And it begins with you deciding that your voice, your expertise, and your leadership matter — because they do.

THE DIETITIAN REVOLUTION MANIFESTO

This is the decade of the dietitian. The decade we reclaim healthcare through food, science, and compassion.

Healthcare is broken. Chronic disease is rising.
Patients are drowning in prescriptions while prevention is ignored.

And while we've been busy changing lives one patient at a time, others have been redefining our profession without us:

Venture-backed startups are scaling fast, commoditizing dietitians.
Private equity is consolidating practices and dictating care.
Insurers are prioritizing efficiency over outcomes.
Legislators are rewriting healthcare policy without our voices in the room.

If we don't act now, we risk becoming replaceable.
But if we unite, innovate, and lead, we can take back control.

Our Belief

Food is medicine.
Dietitians are essential providers.
Preventative care belongs to us.

We are the clinicians trained to prevent, reverse, and manage chronic disease through personalized, evidence-based care.

Dietitians are where science becomes care: blending evidence with empathy, data with deep listening, and nourishment with humanity.

We are the future of healthcare.

Our Mission

To reclaim our power as registered dietitians and lead the shift to food-first, preventative medicine.

We will build innovative, high-touch care models that deliver real outcomes.

We will leverage technology on our terms — to enhance, not replace, human connection.

We will pool our data and results to prove our value to payers, employers, and policymakers.

We will protect our scope of practice and advocate for fair reimbursement.

We will unite as a profession to lead the preventative medicine revolution — not follow it.

Our Commitment

We commit to collaboration, not competition — because together, we are stronger.

We commit to bold innovation — designing care models that startups can't replicate.

We commit to fierce advocacy — for ourselves, our patients, and our profession.

We commit to relentless education — elevating public understanding of why dietitians matter.

We commit to unapologetic leadership — claiming our seat at the head of the healthcare table.

This Is Our Moment

The disruption is already here.
But this time, we are the disruption.

We will own the future of preventative medicine.
We will redefine healthcare.
And we will do it together.

ADDITIONAL RESOURCES
FROM THE DIETITIAN REVOLUTION

The Dietitian's Toolkit

The Dietitian's Toolkit serves as a practical resource hub to help readers and listeners implement the ideas, strategies, and frameworks from the book. These materials are designed to make innovation actionable — giving dietitians the tools they need to build, scale, and lead in a rapidly evolving healthcare landscape. These resources can be found at https://rinutritiontherapy.com/dietitian-revolution.

Use the QR code below to easily access the free resources available at *The Dietitian Revolution:*

The Dietitian Revolution

ACKNOWLEDGEMENTS

Jay Hackleman, my dad — You were the first nutrition advocate I ever knew. You instilled in our family the importance of diet and physical activity as the keys to a long and healthy life. We had such a good start because of you. I love that you still send me articles and recommend books about the latest discoveries in nutrition. Sometimes, I think you know more about it than I do. But most importantly, I'm grateful you're my dad. You are a good man with a good heart, and I'm so thankful for you.

Lori Mollo & Kristin MacRae, my leading ladies — I am endlessly grateful for your trust, passion, hard work and loyalty. Thank you for believing in me. I could never have built this business without you. I love what we have created, alongside an amazing team: a business built on integrity, courage, honesty and good ol' grit. You have helped me grow in ways I could never have imagined, both personally and professionally. I believe God brought us together to do His work — and I have no doubt He is pleased with what we do and who we are.

Jack, Elena, Tegan & Max, my children — You are the reason I kept going when it would have been easier to give up. You gave me the strength to build a foundation of financial security, independence, and stability. You've taught me how to live my life through a lens of legacy: to live every day with courage, resilience, thoughtfulness and authenticity. Bringing your lives into this world — gave me life. There is no greater gift I have been given in this life — than yours. Everything I continue to build — for myself, for this profession, and for the future — began with you.

ABOUT THE AUTHOR

Wendy Leonard, MS, RDN, LDN is a visionary leader and passionate advocate for transforming healthcare through food, lifestyle medicine, and innovation. She is the Founder and CEO of Rhode Island Nutrition Therapy (RINT), one of the region's most dynamic group dietetics practices, known for their hybrid 1:1 and group MNT model.

When she's not working on the business or advocating for the future of dietetics, she enjoys traveling to Iceland (the most peaceful place on earth) and spending time with her husband, friends and her kids.